HOW TO PREPARE FOR

HARD
TIMES

AND PERSECUTION

HOW TO PREPARE FOR

HARD TIMES

AND PERSECUTION

MARIA KNEAS

LIGHTHOUSE TRAILS PUBLISHING
EUREKA, MONTANA

How to Prepare for Hard Times and Persecution
©2015 by Maria Kneas
1st Lighthouse Trails Edition; 2nd printing August 2015
Revised and expanded edition from *Prepare for Persecution*
Published by:
Lighthouse Trails Publishing
P.O. Box 908
Eureka, MT 59917

Library of Congress Cataloging-in-Publication Data

Kneas, Maria M.
  How to prepare for hard times and persecution / Maria Kneas.
    pages cm
  Includes bibliographical references and index.
  ISBN 978-1-942423-02-7 (softbound : alk. paper) 1.
Persecution. 2. Suffering--Religious aspects--Christianity. 3.
United States--Church history--21st century. I. Title.
  BR1601.3.K54 2015
  272'.9--dc23
                                          2015010661

Printed in the United States of America

Dedicated to my husband Ray who is in Heaven. Like the apostle Paul, Ray fought a good fight, and he kept the faith (2 Timothy 4:7). And like Eric Liddell, the Olympic runner, Ray ran with patience the race that was set before him (Hebrews 12:1). May we do the same.

Eric Liddell in his winning Olympic run

Also by Maria Kneas

Strength for Tough Times
Overcoming Obstacles to Trusting the Lord

Contents

Yea, though I walk
through the valley
of the shadow of death,
I will fear no evil:
for thou art with me;
thy rod and thy staff
they comfort me.

(Psalm 23:4)

PREFACE

Many Christians sense we are coming under troubling times including persecution, but they only see bits and pieces of the problems. They have an uneasiness but don't really know why.

North America is in the early stages of persecution, and it is visibly increasing. Some pastors are already saying we are heading for full-blown persecution. Christians need to become spiritually and emotionally prepared for hard times and persecution.

It is common to hear Christians from nations where persecution is taking place say, "We never thought it could happen here" and "Why didn't anybody prepare us?"

It is my hope and prayer that this book will give you valuable information that will help prepare you, as a Christian believer, both spiritually and emotionally for dealing with hard times and persecution. When the world tries to pressure us to deny our Christian faith or to do things that go against biblical standards of morality, then we need to stand our ground and refuse to compromise. We need to have spiritual backbone. We need to stand firm in our faith.

Psalm 2 is a good description of what is going on in the world today. Its relevance will be even more clear if you see the word "king" as including presidents, prime ministers, international "banksters," power elites, etc. The psalm says:

> Why do the heathen rage, and the people imagine a vain thing? The kings of the earth set themselves, and the rulers take counsel together, against the LORD, and against his anointed. (Psalm 2:1-2)

Throughout history, there have been those who have conspired to eliminate God's people. This rebellion takes different forms in different cultures and periods of history. Today, modern technology is involved, but the spirit behind the rebellion against God and the hostility towards His people is the same. Unless they repent and turn to God, these rebels will come to a bad end:

> Thou shalt break them with a rod of iron; thou shalt dash them in pieces like a potter's vessel. (Psalm 2:9)

In contrast, those who are faithful to God will rejoice for all eternity:

> **But as it is written, Eye hath not seen, nor ear heard, neither have entered into the heart of man, the things which God hath prepared for them that love him. (1 Corinthians 2:9)**

1

UNDERSTANDING THE TIMES

I was the first Christian in my family. Around 1982, Mom and Dad (who were in their mid-sixties) began reading the Bible. They became so excited they eagerly devoured it. Dad would come running into the room saying, "Look at this!" and share a Scripture passage that really hit him.

As my parents shared their new-found enthusiasm for the Bible, their love bloomed. They enjoyed *Prairie Home Companion*, and when old timey music came on the radio, Dad would grab Mom and dance with her. He was always bringing her flowers from their garden.

They found a good church where the preaching was biblical. Dad's enthusiasm for Scripture kept growing, and he got a master's degree in Biblical Studies. For the rest of their lives, Mom and Dad read a lot of Scripture every day and often talked about it during meal time.

Sadly, times have changed. If Mom and Dad had discovered the Bible in 2014, they would probably have had difficulty finding a church with biblical preaching. And the last time I listened to *Prairie Home Companion*, the humor had become raunchy.

People on TV now boast about doing things you could have blackmailed them for thirty years ago. Previously "unthinkable" things are becoming commonplace.

This didn't just happen by chance. I'm going to give you some disturbing information, accompanied by this biblical reminder. Jesus told us to love our enemies and to pray for them (Matthew 5:44). We should also do reasonable things to protect ourselves and to try to thwart their anti-Christian agenda, because Jesus told us to flee persecution when we can (Matthew 10:23). But that only applies if we can do it without denying our Lord (Matthew 10:32-33).

Humanism is the mortal enemy of Christianity. It denies the existence of God and opposes biblical morality.

Humanism says that man is basically good, but the Bible says we are all sinners who need a Savior. We need to have God change our hearts. We need to become children of God.

Dr. Brock Chisholm is a psychiatrist. He was the first Secretary-General of the United Nations' World Health Organization. He demonstrated humanism's antipathy to the idea that men need a Savior when he said:

> For many generations we have bowed our necks to the yoke of the conviction of sin. We have swallowed all manner of poisonous certainties fed us by our parents.[1]

> If the race is to be freed from its crippling burden of good and evil, it must be psychiatrists who take the original responsibility.[2]

Evidently, for Dr. Chisholm, "mental health" means being unable to become convicted of sin, and it also means being unable to recognize the difference between good and evil. According to American law, the inability to tell the difference between good and evil is the definition of "criminal insanity."

Dr. Chisholm made these statements in 1946. Therefore, the United Nations has had many years to try to change every country in ways that make it more difficult for its citizens to recognize the difference between good and evil. That could explain a lot of the crazy things we see going on in the world today.

In America, humanism has been declared by the courts to be a tax-exempt religion.[3] This religion is openly hostile to Christianity. Its antagonism can be seen in the following quotations from humanists:

> The classroom must and will become the arena of conflict between the old and the new—the rotting corpse of Christianity . . . and the new faith of humanism.[4]

> Some opponents of Humanism have accused us of wishing to overthrow the traditional Christian family. They are right. That is exactly what we intend to do.[5]

In 1933, *The Humanist Manifesto* was written, stating the beliefs and goals of humanism.[6] One of the signers was John Dewey, who is called the "father of progressive education." He revolutionized education in America. Dewey was determined to use the school system to promote humanism.[7] Unfortunately, he succeeded.

For generations, American children have been taught humanist beliefs and values in public schools. Their Christian morals have been undermined by "values clarification" and other techniques.[8] Thomas Sowell said:

american children have been taught humanist beliefs and values in public schools— their christian morals have been undermined by "values clarification" and other techniques

The techniques of brainwashing developed in totalitarian countries are routinely used in psychological conditioning programs imposed on American school children.[9]

This results in radically changing the beliefs and moral values of the children. The brainwashing techniques result in "acceptance of alternative values by psychological rather than rational means."[10]

In addition, there are people who call themselves atheists, but they hate God. (How can they hate somebody who doesn't exist? At some level, they must know God is real.)

Look at the following quotation from 1977. The militant atheists have been working on this agenda for a long time now:

> We must ask how we can kill the God of Christianity. We need only to insure that our schools teach only secular knowledge.[11]

With such overt hostility to Christianity from humanists and atheists, who use the public schools to promote their agenda, it is not surprising that America has gone downhill spiritually and morally. For example, when I was in high school (1958-1961), there were only a few girls who were not virgins, and everybody knew who they were. They had "a reputation." Fast-forward forty years to the year 2000 when my nephew got married. He and his wife were both virgins, and that was so unusual that people made a big deal out of it.

To see the extent of the change that has taken place in the United States, look at Yale University. It was founded by ministers in 1701 in order to spread Christianity. All students were required to "live religious, godly, and blameless lives according to the rules of God's Word." They were told to spend time in prayer and reading Scripture, both publicly and in private. The stated goal of their studies was "to know God in Jesus Christ" and "to lead a godly, sober life."[12]

And what is Yale like today in modern America? In March 2013, students at Yale University attended a four-day workshop called "Sex Weekend." This event was led by a "sexologist," who gave the students "sensitivity training" in "sexual diversity." The students were taught to accept homosexuality, sadomasochism, bestiality (sex with animals), incest, and prostitution. Over half of Yale's students said they had engaged in "consensual pain" (sadomasochism), and three percent said they had sex with an animal.[13]

With humanists using the schools to try to undermine Christianity, it is not surprising that many people who were raised in Christian families do not share the faith of their parents and grandparents. According to one study, the majority of today's young adults were involved in church and other Christian activities as teenagers. However, when they grew older, most of them became "spiritually disengaged." Among young adults who had a Christian background, only one out of five "maintained a level of spiritual activity consistent with their high school experiences."

This study also showed that three out of four American teenagers have engaged in "psychic or witchcraft-related activity." (This does not include reading horoscopes and exposure to occult media.) One out of ten participated in a seance, and one out of twelve tried to cast a spell or mix a magic potion. More than a third used a Ouija board, and more than a third read a book about Wicca (a religion based on witchcraft and goddess worship).[14] Occultism is becoming mainstream.

Things have now gotten to the point that there is a movement to normalize pedophilia. Instead of wanting to protect children from sexual predators, some psychologists and academics want to protect the sexual rights of pedophiles, which they have rebranded as being "minor-attracted persons" who have a sexual orientation that should be respected.[15]

As a result of America's moral and spiritual free fall, we now see blatant hostility towards Christianity. For example, in 2001, a man in my church was sent to prison. Some of us visited him and asked if we could give him a magazine. The prison officials told us we could do that, as long as it came directly from the publisher and the magazine was "appropriate." I asked them what "appropriate" meant and was told that pornography and violent material were not allowed.

We subscribed to a Christian magazine to be sent to him directly by the publisher. The prison refused that magazine and sent it back. Evidently, somebody at that prison considered Christian writings to be "inappropriate." They treated it the same way they treat pornography, by refusing to let him have it.

I talked about this with a friend from church whose son was in prison. She told me her son was not allowed to have a Bible. His prison was full of Muslim literature and Wiccan writings, but Bibles were not allowed.

Some persecution takes the form of pressuring people to do things contrary to their religious convictions. For example, a Catholic nurse was forced to assist in performing an abortion. If she refused, she would be fired. She complied, but regrets it and is now suing the hospital. This is part of a larger problem. The ACLU is trying to force Catholic hospitals to perform abortions.[16]

Sixty-three businesses have lawsuits about provisions in ObamaCare that would force them to go against their religious convictions. One attorney said:

> The United States government is taking the remarkable position that private individuals lose their religious freedom when they make a living.[17]

Jack Phillips is a Christian baker from Denver, Colorado. He politely refused to bake a wedding cake for a homosexual couple, saying he would be happy to bake things for them "for any other occasion." There were demonstrations outside his shop, and he received so many death threats he called the police. Then the couple charged him with discrimination. The judge ruled that if he refuses to make wedding cakes for homosexual marriages, he will be fined, and he might be sent to prison. The baker said he would rather go to jail than violate his religious beliefs.[18]

Elaine and Jonathan Huguenin are Christians and the owners of Elane Photography. In 2006, they turned down a request to do wedding photos for a same-sex marriage. This case went all the way to the New Mexico Supreme Court, which ruled against them. One of the judges said the Huegenins are "compelled by law to compromise the very religious beliefs that inspire their lives." Their attorney said:

> If Elane Photographer does not have her rights of conscience protected, then basically nobody does. . . . Americans are now on notice that the price of doing business is their freedom.[19]

If such things can be done to bakers and photographers and florists, then what will happen to pastors and other religious clergy who refuse to marry homosexual couples? What will happen to freedom of religion?

Using the courts to try to force people to endorse homosexuality is done by militant homosexual activists. These radical activists want to force everybody else to actively support what they are doing.

In contrast, that baker had turned down requests for wedding cakes from a number of other homosexual couples who respected his right to see things differently than they do. They just quietly looked for another baker who would be happy to get their business.

When I was a freshman in college (1961-1962), I had a friend there named Jessica. She was bisexual. Back then, I had never heard that term before. I didn't even know that such a thing existed before I became friends with her.

She was desperately looking for love and had become promiscuous. Men would use her and treat her like trash. When that became too painful, then Jessica would turn to women. But then she would get hurt by them and go back to men again. It was a cycle of pain, going back and forth between men and women and getting hurt by them all.

Jessica was a sweet, vulnerable girl, and her heart was broken by so many people. I wish I could have helped her back then, but I didn't know how. If Jessica married a lesbian, she would never try to force a baker to make a wedding cake for her. She cared about other people, and respected them.

I've often thought about Jessica over the years and prayed for her. I hope she found the Lord.

During the 2014 U.S. government shutdown, the military chaplains were banned from performing any kind of services or ministry on military bases. They were not even allowed to minister as volunteers (which would not have cost the Pentagon a penny), and they were threatened with arrest if they did any ministry on base. Congressman Tim Huelskamp said:

> Time and time again this Administration demonstrates it is waging a war against the very religious freedoms upon which America was founded.[20]

Obviously, this had nothing to do with saving money, because the chaplains offered to serve for free as volunteers. In addition, it costs money to arrest people and hold them in jail, and it is expensive to have lawyers prosecute them. So this was overt persecution of Christians. And it was done by our government to the men and women who risk life and limb in order to protect our nation and who also risk having post-traumatic stress, which is very difficult to live with.

The Pentagon has threatened to court martial soldiers who share their faith. This includes military chaplains.[21]

On March 21, 2014, the Family Research Council published a report titled *A Clear and Present Danger: The Threat to Religious Liberty in the Military*. It is 21 pages long and very thoroughly documented. You can get a free PDF file of it online.[22]

There have been some cases where American Christians have been murdered for their faith. On September 15, 1999, there was a rally at Wedgewood Baptist Church in Fort Worth, Texas. A gunman entered the church and methodically shot Christians who were attending the service and then shot himself. Seven people died and others were critically wounded. The gunman was shouting, cursing Christianity, and cursing the Christians for believing it. The FBI found anti-Christian writings in his home.[23]

However, in spite of this evidence, when CBS and CNN reported the shooting, they were "unable to assign any motive to the shooter."[24] Why? Because it is not politically correct to portray Christians as being persecuted. The mainstream media avoids such stories or else covers them in ways that omit or deny the element of persecution. I found out about that twenty years ago when I learned that Christians in Sudan were being slaughtered by Muslims. I contacted every newspaper I knew to tell them about it. None of them responded, with one exception. One reporter told me, "I wish I could write about it." So evidently he wanted to cover the story but was not allowed to.

On April 20, 1999, two students at Columbine High School in Littleton, Colorado shot and killed twelve of their classmates and a teacher, and wounded 23 other people. They also killed themselves. They asked three Christian girls if they believed in God and killed them when they said "Yes." The girls were Cassie Bernall, Rachel Scott, and Valeen Schnurr. Rachel had shared her Christian faith with the boys several weeks earlier. (Some classmates overheard the conversation.) The boys made a video in which they cursed Jesus Christ and cursed Christians. They singled Rachel Scott out for an insulting tirade, mocking her by name.[25]

I read about the shootings in the newspaper, but those reports didn't mention the element of persecuting Christian students. It took me years to find out about that, and I got the information from a story on a Christian website about Rachel Scott's father. I never heard anything about it from the mainstream media. Did you?

And this is the condemnation, that light is come into the world, and men loved darkness rather than light, because their deeds were evil. For every one that doeth evil hateth the light . . . But he that doeth truth cometh to the light, that his deeds may be made manifest. (John 3:19-21)

Then Nebuchadnezzar in his rage and fury commanded to bring Shadrach, Meshach, and Abendego. Then they brought these men before the king. Nebuchadnezzar . . . said unto them, Is it true, O Shadrach, Meshach, and Abednego, do not ye serve my gods, nor worship the golden image which I have set up? Now if ye be ready . . . ye fall down and worship the image which I have made; well: but if ye worship not, ye shall be cast the same hour into the midst of a burning fiery furnace; and who is that God that shall deliver you out of my hands?

Shadrach, Meshach, and Abednego, answered and said to the king, O Nebuchadnezzar . . . If it be so, our God whom we serve is able to deliver us from the burning fiery furnace, and he will deliver us out of thine hand, O king. But if not, be it known unto thee, O king, that we will not serve thy gods, nor worship the golden image which thou hast set up. (Daniel 3:13-18)

2

BRAINWASHING CHRISTIANS?

I n the first chapter, I told you about Jack Phillips, the owner of Masterpiece Cake Shop in Denver, Colorado. He was threatened with fines and possibly prison because he refused to bake a wedding cake for a homosexual couple. He said he would rather go to prison than compromise his faith and his moral convictions.

He was able to avoid prison and the fines by deciding to never bake any more wedding cakes again. He can't be accused of discriminating if nobody gets his wedding cakes. That keeps him out of prison, but it makes it much more difficult for him to earn a livelihood. In addition, wedding cakes are his specialty and his passion, a form of artistic expression. He has a gift for doing them beautifully, and he loves making them.

This case took another turn which is very disturbing. The Colorado Civil Rights Commission has ordered Phillips and all of his staff (which includes his 87-year-old Christian mother) to submit to a regimen of "sensitivity training." This is to make sure that Phillips and every single person working for him agrees with their interpretation of Colorado's non-discrimination statute. In other words, they are trying to force Phillips and his staff to believe it is right and proper for them to bake wedding cakes for homosexual couples.

When the judge ordered him to bake wedding cakes for homo-sexual couples, Phillips said:

> That violates my First Amendment . . . and my duty as a Christian abiding by my Savior.[1]

Phillips also said that, if necessary, he would be willing to go to prison because of his convictions. He stated:

> I'm not giving up my faith for anything. It's too high a price to pay.[2]

Phillips has been represented by Alliance Defending Freedom (ADF), which is a conservative advocacy group. Nicolle Martin of ADF said:

> Colorado has no business forcing Jack to abandon deeply held convictions . . . which are protected by the First Amendment, *so the state can impose a new, government-approved belief system upon him.*[3] (emphasis added)

Kristen Waggoner, ADF's Senior Vice President of Legal Services, explained:

> If the government can take away our First Amendment freedoms, there is no other thing it can't take away.[4]

Lee Duigon has an article about this titled, "When the State Owns Your Soul." He begins it by saying:

> Sometimes violence, even murder, isn't the worst thing you can do to a fellow human being. Stealing his soul, taking over the management of his conscience and his mind—those are worse.[5]

This appears to be precisely what the Colorado Civil Rights Commission is attempting to do to Phillips, his elderly mother, and his employees. It also sets a precedent probably intended to intimidate other Christian businessmen.

In addition, if they can force Christians to act against their conscience and convictions, then they can do similar things to other groups of people. For example, could black businessmen be required to provide services for KKK functions? Could Jewish businessmen be required to provide services for the Muslim Brotherhood or other anti-Semitic groups?

Phillips and his mother will never agree with the judge's interpretation of Colorado's non-discrimination statute. They will insist they have a right and a duty to act according to their conscience, which is guided by their Christian faith and by statements in the Bible.

Does this mean that Colorado will require them to keep on taking "sensitivity training" for the rest of their lives, because they have not been "rehabilitated" from their religious beliefs?

> **if they can force christians to act against their conscience and convictions, then they can do similar things to other groups of people**

Whether or not the state of Colorado winds up trying to push it that far, this is a serious issue. It is about brainwashing. It is about denying freedom of religion and freedom of conscience.

The New York State Division of Human Rights is doing the same thing to the Giffords, who are Christian farmers in Schaghticoke, New York. In addition to farming, they also open their home for weddings and receptions, and in 2014, they refused to do it for a lesbian couple who wanted to get married there. The state of New York is forcing the Giffords and their staff to take "re-education" classes in order to change their religious and moral convictions.[6]

The Human Rights Commission in Lexington, Kentucky has done the same thing to Blaine Adamson for not printing shirts promoting the Gay Pride Festival in Lexington. His refusal was not based on the people who requested his business. Instead, it was "because of the message that the shirts would communicate."

His attorney said:

> No one should be forced by the government or by another citizen to endorse or promote ideas with which they disagree.[7]

Since this is happening in three different states within a few months, it looks as if we are likely to see more cases like these. This could become a national trend.

I know a pastor who for years has been saying that at some point, we are going to have to choose whether to worship God or Caesar (i.e., the state). Right now, the state of Colorado is attempting to force this baker and his employees to worship Caesar—to allow the state to override their conscience and their religious convictions.

That is what Hitler did to the Germans and what Marx and Stalin did to the Russians.

As Christians we must be determined to be faithful to God, to live biblically, and to follow our conscience no matter what it costs. We cannot afford to compromise. There is too much at stake:

For what is a man profited, if he shall gain the whole world, and lose his own soul? or what shall a man give in exchange for his soul? (Matthew 16:26)

24

3

THOUGHT POLICE IN COLLEGES

Some universities in the United States are subjecting their students to a form of mind control that includes redefining words. The following quotation from L. Ron Hubbard (the founder of the Scientology cult) describes the procedure for doing this:

> The way to redefine a word is to get the new definition repeated as often as possible . . . A consistent, repeated effort is the key to any success with this technique of propaganda.[1]

A quotation from the University of Delaware demonstrates how they are applying these principles:

> A racist is one who is both privileged and socialized on the basis of race by a white supremacist (racist) system. The term applies to all white people . . . living in the United States.[2]

The University of Delaware has about 7,000 students living on campus. It requires all of these students "to adopt highly specific university approved views on issues ranging from politics to race, sexuality, sociology, moral philosophy and environmentalism." The students are "pressured or even required" to make statements that comply with the school's views.[3]

Being quiet about their beliefs isn't enough to keep students out of trouble. They are interviewed, one on one, with intrusive questions. If students fail to give politically correct answers, then a report is written about them, and the students are subjected to "treatment," namely compulsory re-education.

This is a state university, which means that it is supported by taxes. Therefore, people who would be appalled by such things are required by law to support them financially.

The Foundation for Individual Rights in Education (FIRE) has produced a video about this brainwashing. In interviews with students and professors, it shows how the university's Office of Residence Life used a variety of methods to "coerce students to change their thoughts, values, attitudes, beliefs, and habits" so they would "conform to a highly specified social, environmental, and political agenda."[4]

One of the university's views is that all whites of European descent are, by definition, racists. That would include William Wilberforce, a white Englishman who spent his life working for the abolition of slavery.[5]

Is this hard to believe? Then read these current definitions from the University of Delaware Office of Residence Life Diversity Facilitation Training:

> A RACIST: [A]ll white people . . . By this definition, people of color cannot be racists, because as peoples within the U.S. system, they do not have the power to back up their prejudices. (page 3)

> A NON RACIST: A non term. The term was created by whites to deny responsibility for systemic racism. (page 3)

The "racist" label would apply to James Reeb, because he was a white American man. He was beaten to death by segregationists on March 11, 1965, because he participated in Rev. Dr. Martin Luther King Jr.'s march for civil rights in Selma, Alabama.[6]

It would also include my friend Sheila, a white woman who also participated in that civil rights march in Selma. Although timid by nature, Sheila could be strong when it came to standing up for what she believed in. She risked her life to participate in that march, and she had to face police dogs and cattle prods. But the University of Delaware says that Sheila is a racist because she is white.

It would also include white couples who adopt black children. And it would include whites who marry blacks. According to the university, these people are, by definition, racists—no matter how they behave, and no matter what they believe.

So according to the University of Delaware, "racism" has little or nothing to do with behavior, beliefs, and motives. It is all about the university's philosophy and ideology. What men and women actually think, and how they actually behave, is irrelevant.

There was strong resistance to this program at the University of Delaware. As a result, it was discontinued in October 2007.[7] But in May 2008, the program was revived. And it still has the same definition of racism.[8]

The University of Minnesota has proposed a similar program. It apparently intends to change its admissions process in order to screen out potential students who have "wrong" beliefs and values. Present students whose beliefs don't conform to the university's ideology, and who do not change their beliefs as a result of mandatory re-education, would not be able to get degrees. In other words, after successfully completing their studies, they would be refused the degree they earned because of their personal beliefs.[9]

This program of indoctrination is especially aimed at future teachers. The Teacher Education Redesign Initiative is a group whose objective is to "change the way future teachers are trained" at the University of Minnesota. It requires teachers to embrace (and teach) its worldview, which sees America as being "an oppressive hellhole: racist, sexist and homophobic."[10]

Many American colleges are indoctrinating students instead of educating them. This widespread problem is documented in Jim Nelson Black's book *Freefall of the American University: How Our Colleges Are Corrupting the Minds and Morals of the Next Generation.*

This process involves coercion, mind control, and the unconstitutional lack of free speech and freedom of conscience. It also involves "service learning"—sending students into troubled neighborhoods where they are trained to justify immorality and despise traditional values. What does this do to the ability of students to think logically and to deal with objective facts?

Replacing real education with indoctrination creates a generation of students whose beliefs and behavior are ruled by propaganda and feelings instead of facts and logical thinking. These victims of contemporary brainwashing can easily be manipulated by clever slogans, clever music, and clever TV ads. This is a perfect setup for power hungry politicians.

Back in the fifties, countless Western prisoners of war faced communist brainwashing in Asia and the Soviet Union. Only those prisoners whose faith and values were anchored in unwavering truth were able to resist the disorienting assaults on their minds. Genuine Christians demonstrated a spiritual resistance that baffled Communist change agents and even converted guards.

Never has it been more important to stand firm in God's Word, train our children to reject compromise, and stand together in God-given strength as we face a world that hates our values and mocks our God!

The LORD is on my side; I will not fear:
what can man do unto me? (Psalm 118:6)

4

TEACHING KIDS TO BE SOCIOPATHS

n chapter one, I told how some humanists are trying to destroy people's ability to tell the difference between right and wrong. In addition, brain-washing techniques are being used on school children in order to change their moral values. What are the results of such things in real life?

Here is one example. It involves black students, but it has absolutely nothing to do with racism. I was a civil rights activist back in the days of Martin Luther King, Jr. These are facts that show something about the state of many of our young people, regardless of race. In April 2013, there was a race riot in Virginia Beach. There was widespread violence and destruction by black college students who were "having fun." This involved forty thousand college students. That is a huge number of people. It's like a full-fledged invasion.[1]

Their "fun" included destroying a small family business that had taken a lifetime to build. It was the kind of small place that gets "regulars," where people know each other.

That "fun" also resulted in three stabbings, three shootings, and numerous beatings—one so severe that it resulted in bleeding in the brain. These college students were terrifying people "for fun." All of the victims were white, and all of the perpetrators were black.

These were not gang youth. And they were not poor, oppressed, deprived, inner-city kids. These were college-age adults. Most of them had enough education and enough money to be able to go to college.

The destruction and violence wasn't based on anger due to some kind of Rodney King incident or anything like that. It was just a bunch of college kids "having fun."

This reminds me of the video of college students having "fun" at a birthday party by playing a game called "abortion battles." Pairs of boys put balloons underneath their shirts, pretending to be pregnant. They attacked each other's bellies with forks, trying to pop those balloons. And the party crowd was laughing and cheering them on, yelling things like, "Kill that baby!" These were college students, mostly white, and girls as much as boys. (You can see a video of this on YouTube.)[2]

It also reminds me of some teens who gang raped a girl. Then they laughed and said things like, "She is so raped!" They also urinated on that girl and bragged about it, laughing as they did. (You can see a video of their bragging on YouTube.)[3]

Likewise, something happened back in the days when I was a temporary secretary, going from place to place. In one office, I worked with a young woman who cheerfully told me she had deliberately gotten pregnant in order to see if she was able to. Then she had an abortion because she didn't want to have a baby. She deliberately murdered a baby in order to find out if she was fertile.

She told me about this in a most pleasant manner, as part of light conversation, as if what she had done was normal behavior. Here again, we are not talking about some poor, disadvantaged, uneducated person. We are talking about a secretary—a professional with education and special training.

For years, our public schools have been promoting "values clarification" and teaching children there are no moral absolutes—that objective truth does not exist. That there is no such thing as objective right and wrong. The behavior I describe above is the fruit of that teaching.

The definition of being "criminally insane" is being unable to tell the difference between right and wrong. So we are literally teaching school kids to become criminally insane. Or to put it another way, we are teaching them to become sociopaths.

There is a TV channel called Nickelodeon. Years ago, it had reruns of good old fashioned, clean cut shows like *Leave it to Beaver*. Parents believed their children could safely watch this channel because of the shows it carried. However, between the segments of the shows, they had quick skits showing kids with total disrespect for their parents and things like that. Perhaps you could call those "commercials for a spirit of lawlessness."

They also had a game show. I saw one episode of it. They took two teams of school children and put them in rooms (nice rooms, with nice things in them). The aim of the game was to totally trash the rooms as quickly and as thoroughly as they could. There was upbeat music playing while they did it, and the audience was laughing and cheering. The team that trashed their room the fastest won a prize.

That game was teaching those kids to do exactly what those college students did to that family business in Virginia Beach. And it was teaching that lesson to middle class youth in nice homes, in nice neighborhoods, all over America.

For these kids, the people they are hurting don't seem like real people to them. They see them as being just props on their stage—objects to be used or characters in a video game they are playing. These young people are acting like sociopaths. And our public schools have taught them to be that way; so have Hollywood and the music industry.

To that mix, add the fact that many colleges today are teaching that, by definition, every white person is a racist and that racism doesn't depend on what people say, or what they do, or how they think. According to those colleges, just having white skin, by definition, makes people racists. (See chapter three, "Thought Police in Colleges.") Therefore, the teachings of those colleges encouraged those black students to attack, terrify, and vandalize white people in Virginia Beach.

We know that the Nazis and the Communists did things that were cruel and destructive. Some of them were overtly evil people, and they knew exactly what they were doing. However, for many of them, that was not their original intention. They had been taught that what they were doing would lead to a utopia, to a better world for themselves and for their children. They saw themselves as doing something necessary in order to bring about the utopia they longed for. Hard-core Communists refer to such people as "useful idiots."

Because they had a conscience, the "useful idiots" had to be deceived in order to get them to do bad things. It took a lot of clever propaganda, shameless lying, and brainwashing techniques in order to get them to the point where they would call evil good, and call good evil, and act accordingly. They were taught that what they were doing would lead to a "greater good," to a better world. Of course, their thinking was twisted. But because they had been deceived, they thought they were doing the right thing.

What we are seeing in North America has gone even further down the slippery slope. These kids don't have to think that mayhem is for the purpose of creating a "greater good." They will do it just to "have fun"—as if it's just a video game.

Violent video games they play keep reinforcing that. So does the violent rap music or demonic rock music they keep pumping into their heads. And so do MTV's music videos.

Years ago, I once saw one of those MTV music videos when I was visiting somebody in the hospital. He turned off the sound, but I saw an incredible amount of violence and death and occultism, all mixed in with sex. Of course, that associates death and violence with sexual pleasure. It was unspeakably depraved.

Young people like these seem to have no conscience at all. They have become sociopaths. And these college kids will become leaders in society because of their education.

We didn't need to have a Babylonian invasion in order to destroy America. We are doing it to ourselves, from within. And the "cultural Christians" in this nation are allowing it to happen, right under their noses.

As in the days of Elijah, God has a faithful remnant. And He can use even this mess for His glory. He can use it to wake some people up and make them realize they need God. They cannot make it on their own. They desperately need God. Once people understand that, then they will turn to God.

As in the days of the early church (which suffered horrible persecution by the Romans), the true church will grow and get stronger. True Christians will become more serious about God and more devoted to Him and to their brothers and sisters in Christ. What the enemy means for evil, God will use for good.

We are heading for hard times. But individuals who love God and put their trust in Him will come through the refiner's fire as pure gold.

Many shall be purified, and made white, and tried; but the wicked shall do wickedly: and none of the wicked shall understand; but the wise shall understand. (Daniel 12:10)

If my people, which are called by my name, shall humble themselves, and pray, and seek my face, and turn from their wicked ways; then will I hear from heaven, and will forgive their sin, and will heal their land. (2 Chronicles 7:14)

BUT IF YE TURN AWAY, and forsake my statutes and my commandments, which I have set before you, and shall go and serve other gods, and worship them; then will I pluck them up by the roots out of my land which I have given them; and . . . will I cast out of my sight. (2 Chronicles 7: 19-20)

5

A BIBLICAL WARNING FOR AMERICA

The Book of Judges shows a gradual process by which the Israelites (God's chosen people) turned away from God in stages, to follow "other gods" (i.e., the gods of the Canaanites and other pagans).

These stages are not limited to the Israelites. They also apply to Christians, because we are also God's people. Therefore, we should learn from what happened to the Israelites so we won't have to go through the suffering they endured. Here are the stages:

Stage 1. Peace and Prosperity

God blessed His people with peace and prosperity because He loves them. All seemed to be going well for them. They were grateful, and they loved and served God.

Stage 2. Apathy and Compromise

After a while, the people took God's gifts for granted, and they forgot Him. They served Him apathetically, or else they neglected Him altogether. They found reasons for no longer following God:

But this thing commanded I them, saying, Obey my voice, and I will be your God, and ye shall be my people: and walk ye in all the ways that I have commanded you, that it may be well unto you. But they hearkened not, nor inclined their ear, but walked in the counsels and in the imagination of their evil heart, and went backward, and not forward. (Jeremiah 7:23-24)

The next chapter shows how this is happening here in America, and how it happened in Germany before Hitler came to power. There are a number of very troubling parallels.

Stage 3. Rebellion and Paganism

The people turned to other gods for strength and help. The Bible calls that spiritual prostitution. (We see this analogy very clearly in the book of Hosea, where God compares Israel to a faithless wife who leaves her husband and runs after other men.) The Bible says:

And yet they would not hearken unto their judges, but they went a whoring after other gods, and bowed themselves unto them. (Judges 2:17)

God warned them that because they turned away from Him, He would no longer protect them:

The Zidonians also, and the Amalekites, and the Maonites, did oppress you; and ye cried to me, and I delivered you out of their hand. Yet ye have forsaken me, and served other gods: wherefore I will deliver you no more. Go and cry unto the gods which ye have chosen; let them deliver you in the time of your tribulation. (Judges 10:12-14)

Stage 4. Famine, War, Plagues and Slavery

God allowed bad things to happen to His people. They went through great suffering (Jeremiah 6:19).

The Israelites were conquered by outsiders. However, people can also be conquered from within. Hitler was elected as president of Germany. Then he cleverly undermined the freedom of the people and became a full-fledged dictator. He did it incrementally, in stages, and managed to make each stage seem to be reasonable. By the time the people realized what was happening, it was too late.

Stage 5. Confession and Repentance

God showed the people the inadequacy of their own resources, and the fact that pagan gods would not take care of them. They discovered they needed God and needed to be right with Him. They finally repented and confessed their sins:

> O Lord, to us belongeth confusion of face, to our kings, to our princes, and to our fathers, because we have sinned against thee. To the Lord our God belong mercies and forgivenesses, though we have rebelled against him; Neither have we obeyed the voice of the Lord our God, to walk in his laws, which he set before us by his servants the prophets . . . O my God, incline thine ear, and hear; open thine eyes, and behold our desolations, and the city which is called by thy name: for we do not present our supplications before thee for our righteousnesses, but for thy great mercies. O Lord, hear; O Lord, forgive. (Daniel 9:8-10, 18-19)

Stage 6. God Hears, Saves, and Restores

God blesses His people with peace. He protects them and often prospers them—as long as they follow Him.

Where does the United States and the Western world fit in this cycle? Some Christians still believe the Bible and take God seriously and try to live biblically. Unfortunately, they are a minority.

Many people go to church for social or cultural reasons, rather than devotion to God. And many pastors preach a watered-down gospel because they want their listeners to feel good, so that their church will grow big and be successful in worldly terms.

Some pastors deny foundational Christian doctrines, and some bring New Age teachings and practices into their churches. This is described in *A Time of Departing* by Ray Yungen, and *A "Wonderful" Deception* by Warren B. Smith.

That is the second stage: apathy and compromise.

In America, humanism can serve as a bridge between biblical faith and paganism. First, people turn to men as their source of authority, rather than the Bible. Having done that, it is then easier for them to turn to pagan gods. Or, to put it another way, first they make a god out of man, and then they turn to more traditional pagan gods:

> Thus saith the Lord; Cursed be the man that trusteth in man, and maketh flesh his arm, and whose heart departeth from the Lord. (Jeremiah 17:5)

The New Age movement is another bridge between biblical faith and paganism. First, people get into New Age things. Then from there, they can get into overt paganism. (The New Age movement is pagan, but it is dressed up in modern vocabulary and imagery so it isn't obvious.)

Pagan goddess worship has gotten into many mainline churches. In addition, it is being taught in public schools, universities, and nursing schools. It is also being promoted by Hollywood, the music industry, and the media. In addition, practical witchcraft is being taught in some public schools.

According to the Bible, pagan gods and goddesses are demons:

> But I say, that the things which the Gentiles sacrifice, they sacrifice to devils, and not to God: and I would not that ye should have fellowship with devils. (1 Corinthians 10:20)

Wiccan beliefs and practices are getting into mainline denominations. For example, two Methodist clergywomen participated in a croning ritual (a witchcraft initiation ritual). They both wrote articles praising their experience in Wellsprings, a journal for Methodist clergywomen. When contacted by Insight on the News, both women confirmed their participation in the croning ritual, and said that their bishop (a woman) had also participated. When the bishop was contacted, she said that she "witnessed many croning rituals."[1]

That is the third stage: rebellion and paganism.

To get some idea of the degree to which paganism is taking over our society, look at how far we have fallen morally. Pagan morals are directly opposed to biblical morality. Our movies and TV and other entertainment often promote pagan values, and many Christians watch it.

The Canaanites had temple prostitutes, and they were men as well as women, and children as well as adults. As a result, when the Israelites turned to worshiping Canaanite gods, they became promiscuous, they practiced homosexuality, and they had sex with children. In addition, they also killed babies because some of the Canaanite gods (such as Molech) required they sacrifice their babies.

How far has America fallen into paganism? And what are the potential consequences, according to the cycle described in the book of Judges?

In 1950, most people were virgins when they got married. But now that has become rare because sex before marriage has become the norm.

I never even heard of homosexuality until the 1960s, when I befriended a girl in college who turned out to be bisexual. These days, some children are hearing about homosexuality in kindergarten in our public schools. And some school kids are being forced to act like homosexuals. For example, in one school, girls thirteen and fourteen years old were told by their teacher to ask other girls for a lesbian kiss.[2]

Today, children are becoming sexually active at incredibly young ages. For example, two five-year-old children in kindergarten had sex in their classroom's bathroom.[3] Kids in public schools are having sex in the hallways, on the stairs, and even in classrooms.[4] (To see other ways in which many young people have lost their moral compass, see chapter four, "Teaching Kids to be Sociopaths.")

You may think, "Well, at least we don't sacrifice babies to pagan gods." True, but we have killed 55 million babies through abortion.[5] In addition, a woman who is a pagan and a psychologist wrote a book titled *The Sacrament of Abortion*. She calls abortion "a sacred act," a sacrifice to the goddess Artemis (also known as Diana).[6] Are we really any different than those who sacrificed babies to pagan gods?

What about adults having sex with children? Well, some psychologists and academicians are trying to normalize pedophilia. Instead of protecting children from sexual predators, they want to be sensitive to the feelings and sexual orientation of pedophiles, which they have given a name that sounds nicer. They call them "minor-attracted persons."[7]

Another indication (perhaps the biggest of all) of how pagan we have become is the fact that occultism is becoming mainstream. Witchcraft, sorcery, fortune telling, and consulting the dead (necromancy) are strictly forbidden in the Bible. But they have become commonplace. According to one study, three out of four teenagers have engaged in "psychic or witchcraft-related activity." Many of them participated in séances, tried to cast a spell, or mixed a magic potion.[8]

In the Book of Judges, once the nation of Israel worshiped pagan gods and goddesses (which includes rejecting biblical morality in favor of pagan moral standards), then they were heading for judgment. The next thing that happened was famine, war, plagues, and slavery. Could those things happen in America and throughout the Western world?

In the alternative news, I read about the potential for another major war, perhaps even a world war. Food is already more expensive because unusual weather is hurting crops. In addition, bees are dying off, and they are needed to pollinate crops. Some people are afraid that the American dollar will lose its value, resulting is hyperinflation.

The mainstream media often tells us about diseases that have people worried about the possibility of a pandemic. In addition, one out of four teenaged girls in America has at least one sexually transmitted disease.[9]

You may ask, "What about slavery?" Well, if we wind up with a dictatorship, then we could have slave labor. The Nazis had slave labor in their concentration camps. The Russians, Chinese, and North Koreans have it in their labor camps today.

Modern America and Canada have not seen famine or plagues, and our shores have never been invaded (with the exception of Pearl Harbor). And I hope such things will never happen to us. However, we are not immune to them, and we need to be prepared, spiritually.

We have some good, solid Bible-believing Christians in North America. But there were also some faithful Israelites during the time of the Babylonian captivity. Daniel was a godly man, but he had to go into captivity along with his people. And so did Shadrach, Meshach, and Abednego. They suffered a lot because of the sins of their countrymen. The problem was that so much of Israel had abandoned God and turned away to pagan gods. The faithful ones like Daniel were small in number compared to those who went "whoring after other gods" (Judges 2:17).

Even if the people all around us turn away from God and biblical morality, we need to hold on to our integrity. We are doing it for God, not for men. That is part of being faithful to Him.

If our nation suffers because it has turned away from God, then we still need to be faithful to Him. Like Daniel. And like Shadrach, Meshach, and Abednego.

The most important thing is our relationship with God. If we love Him and trust Him, then He will make ALL things work out for our long-term, eternal good (Romans 8:28). We are never at the mercy of men or circumstances, because no matter what happens, God can bring good out of it.

Conversely, for those who don't put their trust in the Lord and love God, nothing will do them any good. Even if they have a pleasant life here on earth, it won't do them any good in the long term because when they die, they will wind up in Hell.

The bottom line is our relationship with God—not our circumstances.

In the musical *Fiddler on the Roof*, Reb Tevye sings a song to his wife: "Do You Love Me?" Well, God has been asking us that question all through history. Every single person who was ever born has to answer that question. And they don't just answer it in words. They answer it by how they live and how they relate to God.

Tragically, although God created people, and He loves them, multitudes have rejected Him. Something else is more important to them. Something else takes first place instead of God. (The Bible calls that idolatry.) Jesus told us:

> Enter ye in at the strait gate: for wide is the gate, and broad is the way, that leadeth to destruction, and many there be which go in thereat: Because strait is the gate, and narrow is the way, which leadeth unto life, and few there be that find it. (Matthew 7:13-14)

God has suffered so much unrequited love. That's all the more reason for us to love Him. He created us so we could love Him. And He loved us first and gave us the ability to love Him back (1 John 4:19). So let's love Him deeply, and faithfully, and consistently. And let's do whatever we can to help others love Him.

Views of the World

Christians' view of the world should be based on the Bible and on their understanding of, and relationship with, the Lord Jesus Christ. However, we live in a world with many other beliefs, values, and ways of thinking.

Christians have a very different worldview from that of pagans and New Agers. They have different approaches to theology, philosophy, psychology, morality, child rearing, and other areas of life.

We need to respect people with other view points because all men and women are created in the image of God (Genesis 1:26-28). In addition, Jesus died for all of us, in order to make it possible for us to become rightly related to God and go to Heaven. If Jesus thinks the people we disagree with are worth dying for, then we should respect them and love them for His sake.

We can love and respect people without agreeing with them. We can even love them when they do things quite hurtful. For example, when Betsie ten Boom was in a Nazi concentration camp, she forgave the Nazi guards who did cruel things to her, and she prayed for them.

Betsie ten Boom

After the war was over, Betsie's sister, Corrie, encountered one of those guards. He had become a Christian after the war and was truly sorry for his past. Corrie was able to love him, in spite of the cruel things he had done in the past. They hugged each other and wept.

When Corrie heard that the man who had betrayed her family was in prison and was going to be executed, she wrote him a letter telling him she forgave him and telling him about the love and forgiveness of Jesus. That man became a Christian before he was killed, and Corrie rejoiced because of it.

Now respecting people with other views of the world does not mean we should compromise our own Christian beliefs. All views are not equal, and all "paths" do not lead to the same place.

For example, if the atheists are right, then when we die, we will all stop existing. If the New Agers and Hindus are right, then when we die, we will be reincarnated. If the Christians are right, then when we die we will go to Heaven, or we will go to Hell.

They cannot all be right, because the end results are so radically different.

As Christians, we need to stand firm in our faith and not apologize for our biblical view of life and the world. We will be vindicated in eternity. In the meantime, we should show love to people who don't know Jesus as their Lord and Savior. And we should pray for their salvation.

On a practical note, loving people does not necessarily mean we trust their judgment. If their moral standards are different from ours, then we should not let them babysit our children. And we would be foolish to be business partners with them. Also, we should not get romantically involved with them. The Bible warns us not to be "unequally yoked" (2 Corinthians 6:14).

We need to protect our children from the influence of such people. And we need to be careful not to allow our faith or our morals to become compromised by them.

Attempts to Blend Christianity with Other Religions

Numerous attempts have been made to blend Christianity with other religions on a world-wide scale. You can read about them in Carl Teichrib's article "Unveiling the Global Interfaith Agenda." [10]

There are also other attempts to merge Christianity with different religions. For example, Chrislam tries to combine Christianity with Islam. [11] There are people who call themselves Christian witches (i.e., combining Christianity with Wicca). There are attempts to mix Christianity with Hinduism, and with Buddhism, and with Shamanism. (A shaman is a Native American medicine man.) Some people claim to be Christian witch doctors or Christian sorcerers. You can even buy a book about Christian Voodoo. [12]

Nominal Christians are people who are Christians in name only. They call themselves Christians, but they really aren't. They don't have a relationship with Jesus Christ, they ignore or deny foundational Christian doctrines, and they don't try to live the way God has instructed us as described in the Bible. Such people can fit in with other religions. However, born-again Christians aren't able to do that because they have God's Spirit living inside them Who convicts them of sin and enables them to trust and obey the Lord. And because God is living inside them, He gives them the grace and strength to abide in Him. Simply put, biblical Christianity cannot mix with other religions.

To compare it to something physical in everyday life, you cannot mix oil and water. Because of their very nature, they just don't mix. You can put them in a glass jar and shake them until they seem to be blended, but then they will separate and the oil will rise to the top of the jar.

To carry that analogy further, if you add an emulsifier, then they can mix. It goes against their nature, but the emulsifier bridges that gap. In real life, Christians who are under severe pressure (such as the threat of prison or torture or death) may go against their nature and try to blend in with whatever is politically correct. That happened in Nazi Germany. I've seen pictures of church altars with swastikas on them. However, Jesus warned us not to make such compromises:

> Whosoever therefore shall confess me before men, him will I confess also before my Father which is in heaven. But whosoever shall deny me before men, him will I also deny before my Father which is in heaven. (Matthew 10:32-33)

These days, it is not politically correct to be "exclusive" by claiming that Jesus Christ is the only way to salvation. However, we need to be biblically correct rather than politically correct. The antidote to the fear of men is the fear of the Lord. Jesus warned us:

> The fear of the Lord is the beginning of knowledge. (Proverbs 1:7)

Jesus made it clear He is the only way to be right with God the Father. There is no other source of salvation. He said:

> I am the way, the truth, and the life: no man cometh unto the Father, but by me. (John 14:6)

> I am the door: by me if any man enter in, he shall be saved, and shall go in and out, and find pasture. The thief cometh not, but for to steal, and to kill, and to destroy: I

am come that they might have life, and that they might have it more abundantly. I am the good shepherd: the good shepherd giveth his life for the sheep. (John 10:7-11)

My Hope is Built on Nothing Less
(by Edward Mote, 1797-1874)

My hope is built on nothing less
Than Jesus' blood and righteousness;
I dare not trust the sweetest frame,
But wholly lean on Jesus' name.
On Christ, the solid Rock, I stand;
All other ground is sinking sand.

When darkness veils His lovely face,
I rest on His unchanging grace;
In every high and stormy gale
My anchor holds within the veil.
On Christ, the solid Rock, I stand;
All other ground is sinking sand.

His oath, His covenant, and blood
Support me in the whelming flood;
When every earthly prop gives way,
He then is all my Hope and Stay.
On Christ, the solid Rock, I stand;
All other ground is sinking sand.

When He shall come with trumpet sound,
Oh, may I then in Him be found,
Clothed in His righteousness alone,
Faultless to stand before the throne!
On Christ, the solid Rock, I stand;
All other ground is sinking sand.

6

HEADING TOWARD DICTATORSHIP

H istory shows us that as free nations become complacent, they become vulnerable to manipulation. Most dictatorships rise gradually—a step at a time. Smooth-talking politicians make each incremental step seem reasonable, because the masses are blind to the tides of change.

We have been warned over and over. But sadly, a time comes when the wisdom of the watchmen is no longer heeded:

> Eternal vigilance is the price of liberty. (Wendell Phillips)

> Giving leaders enough power to create "social justice" is giving them enough power to destroy all justice, all freedom, and all human dignity. (Thomas Sowell)

> Those who cannot remember the past are condemned to repeat it. (George Santayana)

> The greater the power, the more dangerous the abuse. (Edmund Burke)

Austria illustrates the power of gradualism. In 1933, it was a free nation. In 1934, its government began to centralize its power and welcome the influence of Nazi sympathizers. By 1938, it had become a Nazi dictatorship.

The downward slide began with one crisis after another. A third of the people were out of work, inflation rose to 25 percent, and political turmoil caused civil unrest. People longed for a leader to rescue them. Adolf Hitler campaigned in Austria, promising to solve their problems if they were annexed to Germany. A persuasive speaker, he gave them hope and won their hearts. The Austrian people voted him in.[1]

Why? How could the Austrians be so blind? The answer is simple: they faced hard times so they chose to believe Hitler's promises. They didn't see him as we do—brutal, arrogant, narcissistic, and ruthlessly ambitious. That image came later, when it was too late to escape his grasp.

In the beginning, Hitler appeared as a caring, charismatic, captivating visionary.[2] His words brought hope of prosperity, and his public image was intentionally shaped with pictures of his smiles, benevolent deeds and warm encounters with children and babies.[3]

After the annexation, new government jobs were created and order was restored. The people were encouraged and hopeful, and—for a short while—the nation prospered. Then it crashed. This transformation is described by Kitty Werthmann, who lived in Austria when it was ruled by the Nazis:

> Dictatorship did not happen overnight. It was a gradual process starting with national identification cards, which we had to carry with us at all times.[4]

Next came gun registration, followed by attacks on freedom of speech. There were so many informers that people became afraid to say anything political, even when they were in their own homes.

Werthmann tells of other changes, including nationalization of education; indoctrination of children; socialized medicine;

Crowds of people gather in front of and on top of a train to participate in a May Day Nazi party parade (1937—USHMM)

government control of businesses; and a lack of respect for human life. Before the annexation, most Austrian mothers stayed at home to take care of their children. Under Nazi rule, both parents had to work, so the children were sent to government-run daycare centers.

Gun control came in two stages. First there was gun registration, and then the people were required to give up their guns. Once the people were unarmed, they had no way of defending themselves against the Nazis. After that, political correctness replaced freedom of speech; taxes were increased to eighty percent (four fifths of income); the nation was filled with informers; anybody who spoke against the government was arrested; and the people lived in constant fear.

The original caption reads: "One always sees the Fuehrer surrounded by children in pictures."

In Austria, the transformation from freedom to dictatorship was incremental. No nation is immune to such things, including the United States or Canada. In fact, America seems to be following some of the same incremental steps toward totalitarianism.

National Identification Cards

In 2005, the U.S. Congress passed the Real ID Act. This, in effect, would turn drivers' licenses into a national ID card. However, the law is controversial, and seventeen states have passed legislation or resolutions opposing compliance with it.[5]

Congress eventually repealed the law. However, there are ongoing attempts to do similar things but not as comprehensive. According to an article dated March 28, 2013, Senators Chuck Schumer and Lindsey Graham are determined to get a biometric national ID card required for everybody who is employed. And this is so important they met with President Obama to discuss the matter.[6]

WHEN EVIL TAKES OVER

"Brown-shirted storm troopers were marching through the towns, terrorizing everyone and delighting in making life miserable for the Jews, whether by teasing and taunting or by acts of brutality. They ridiculed and beat Jews everywhere and randomly hauled off individuals or families to prison. Cattle cars were filled daily as trainloads of frightened Jews were shipped to secret destinations throughout the tranquil German countryside."

From *Trapped in Hitler's Hell*, the story of Holocaust survivor, Anita Dittman

Nationalizing Education and Indoctrinating Young Children

Kitty Werthmann told us how Hitler nationalized the education system. Christian symbols were removed, and prayer was banned. Through their government-run child-care program, the Nazis would indoctrinate the children with politically correct ideology and absolute loyalty to Hitler. Hitler worship became part of the new structure. The daycare workers were trained in Marxist psychology, not motherly love, for Hitler was fascinated with communist methods of mind control.

Children idolized Hitler and sang his praises. Some American children have been taught to do the same for Obama. I have seen videos of young children singing Obama's praises with adoration and teenagers singing his praises quite militantly. I have also seen a video of a young boy praying to Obama. (Once such videos become controversial, they tend to disappear from YouTube, so you might have difficulty finding them.)

America is also a nation where prayer is no longer allowed in school and even daycare. Obama is centralizing the public schools. His administration is completing a process begun in the nineties during the first Bush administration. A national curriculum with national standards, national tests, and a national database is fast becoming a reality. The goal is to provide "cradle to career education for all of America's children." The federal government is encouraging the states to provide children with "early learning experiences from birth through kindergarten entry."[7]

By imposing government education at such a young age, this system exposes Christian children to the worldviews of secular humanism, neopaganism, and countless other beliefs that clash with home-taught values. It subjects them to anti-Christian peer pressure and to teachers determined to undermine their faith. No wonder children raised in Christian homes from coast to coast are fast rejecting our God and His ways. Meanwhile, churches and youth leaders are bending over backwards to conform to the new values and wants of our youth.

Government schools and the judicial system work hand in hand to undermine the faith of Christian children. For example, Amanda is a ten-year-old Christian homeschooler. She is "well-liked, social and interactive with her peers, academically promising and intellectually at or superior to grade level." Her homeschool curriculum meets all state standards. Yet, a judge has ordered her to attend public school because of her "vigorous defense of her religious beliefs." The judge wants her to consider "different points of view at a time when she must begin to critically evaluate multiple systems of belief."[8] In other words, he is forcing her into government education in order to challenge her Christian faith.

Buried inside the health care bill is a provision giving the federal government control over all student loans. As a result, the government can now decide which students are able to go to college. It can also refuse loans for students who want to attend colleges that the government doesn't approve of, thus putting financial pressure on colleges to be politically correct.[9]

New federal regulations would enable the federal government to control the accreditation of all U.S. colleges. According to former U.S. Senator Bill Armstrong, "the Department of Education is attempting to subject every college and university in America—public and private—to political supervision."[10]

Government Control of Health Care and Businesses

Obama's massive health care bill established government control of health care, which is one sixth of the nation's economy. Its regulation will have a devastating effect on the medical profession. Why would bright students want to invest in medical school when the pay would be minimal and medical "murder" would be mandated? My foot doctor told me, "Obama wants to make me retire early." My general practitioner told me, "Let me take care of you while I still can."

The federal government is wielding an increasing degree of control over businesses, both directly and through regulations. Obama's destructive control over Chrysler has been called "another extraordinary intervention into private industry by the federal government." As a result, many car dealerships were closed.[11] According to an attorney who represents some of those dealers, Chrysler closed them because it was "under enormous pressure from the President's automotive task force."[12]

Treating People Like Livestock

Farmers can kill animals that are born sickly or become too old to be productive. Likewise, Hitler talked about getting rid of "useless eaters." In modern America, some "experts" want to dispose of people with a poor "quality of life."

Jews captured by SS and SD troops during the suppression of the Warsaw ghetto uprising are forced to leave their shelter and march to the Umschlagplatz for deportation. (1943—USHMM)

Kitty Werthmann told how the Nazis killed the mentally challenged people in her village—a result of Hitler's eugenics program. He was following the unconscionable Darwinian ideals of an evolving, purified human race, and he wanted to produce a Master Race of strong, intelligent Aryans. People he considered to be inferior (including Jews and the mentally challenged) had to be eliminated.[13]

Because of the Holocaust, eugenics was discredited. However, euthanasia (both voluntary and involuntary) is spreading. Voluntary euthanasia is a form of suicide, where patients choose to die—usually with a physician's help. This is legal in Oregon and Washington.[14]

Involuntary euthanasia is based on new, convenient medical standards. In Holland, where thousands of patients have been killed against their will, some elderly people are afraid to go to the hospital.[15] A concerned Belgian citizen warned Western nations to guard themselves against "the encroaching euthanasia agenda."[16]

An influential bioethicist in the Obama administration actively promotes health-care rationing.[17] Obama's health-care law includes "death panels" with authority to deny life-saving medical care.[18] Once such care has been denied, it becomes unavailable, even to patients who would pay the cost themselves.

Gun Control

U.S. Attorney General Eric Holder has a long record of supporting gun control. In a 2008 brief to the Supreme Court, Holder claimed that the Second Amendment does not pose any obstacle to banning guns.[19]

Since the shooting at Sandy Hook, the attempts at gun control have increased in both variety and intensity.

Obama initiated a back door approach to gun control by means of an international treaty known as CIFTA. President Clinton signed this treaty in 1997 but the Senate refused to ratify it. Now President Obama is promoting it. According to John Bolton (former U.S. representative of the United Nations):

[T]here's no doubt—as was the case over a decade ago—
that the real agenda is the control of domestic arms.[20]

Enforcing Political Correctness

President Obama co-sponsored a United Nations resolution calling on countries to criminalize "any advocacy of national, racial or religious hatred that constitutes incitement to discrimination, hostility or violence." Since the President of the United States backed the resolution, Americans will be expected to abide by it. As a result, this U.N. resolution would take priority over our constitutional right to free speech.[21]

As a result, people in power can silence those who disagree with them by classifying their statements as "hate speech."

In 2008, a Commissioner of the Federal Communications Commission warned that the FCC is likely to implement regulations that will give the federal government control over the content of radio, TV, and the Internet.[22]

In 2009, a high-ranking official in the FCC called for a "confrontational movement" to increase federal control of the media.[23] He openly expressed admiration for Hugo Chavez' efforts to stifle criticism by seizing control of Venezuela's media.[24]

The chairman of the FCC is "poised to add the Internet to its portfolio of regulated industries."[25] In other words, the media must be controlled by the government:

> Mr. Genachowski suggested that government red tape will increase the 'freedom' of online services that have flourished because bureaucratic busy-bodies have been blocked from tinkering with the Web.[25]

An FCC Commissioner named Michael Copps has proposed a plan: a "public value test" for media. Who will pass that government test? Those who don't will not get their licenses renewed.

Copps declared FCC adoption of his Public Values Test would
provide an antidote to the current state of affairs by requiring:
more diversity . . . enhanced disclosure of information.[26]

This reminds me of the difference between Russian Communism
and Hitler's National Socialism. Stalin ended up with a very poor
country. Hitler's socialism allowed for government controlled "free"
enterprise, and at first it seemed to succeed. The difference between
the two forms of tyrannical socialism was that Stalin's government
owned everything, while Hitler controlled everything.

Informers

In 2002, the federal government attempted to recruit four percent
of the population as informers. These spies were to include people
with access to homes and businesses, such as mailmen, meter readers,
cable installers, and telephone repairmen.[27] After a public outcry,
this plan was abandoned. However, the attempt to have informants
throughout the country is not new. It has continued in various ways,
for years.[28]

As part of former President Bill Clinton's war on "hate crimes,"
the Justice Department had a website that encouraged children to
report relatives who made "derogatory comment[s]."[29] Now that
Congress has passed the "Hate Crimes" bill, we need to be alert to
similar attempts to turn children into informers.

A "Smartphone" is a wireless, pocket-sized computer that also
functions as a cell phone.[30] It can take pictures.[31] The iPhone is a
line of Internet smartphones produced by Apple Computer. People
can get "applications" ("apps") for them, enabling them to do a wide
variety of things, including GPS navigation and social networking.[32]
A person could use his or her iPhone to take a picture, get the precise
location of the place (via GPS), and send the picture and location
information to somebody via e-mail, or post it on the Internet.

A new "app" for iPhones enables citizens to spy on one another
and report directly to several federal agencies, including the FBI

and the Department of Justice.[33] Although this "app" is promoted as a means of preventing terrorism, these spying citizens are also encouraged to report on things such as "environmental negligence" and "discrimination."[34]

The Ability to Arrest People at Will

The President can legally declare a state of national emergency on his own authority without the approval of Congress. There is no legal accountability. Once a national emergency has been declared, the President can "take over all government functions" and "direct all private sector activities" until he declares that the national emergency is over.[35]

A Master Arrest Warrant enables the U.S. Attorney General to have people arrested if he personally considers them to be "dangerous to the public peace and safety." He can keep these people incarcerated indefinitely without legal accountability.[36]

According to a U.S. Congressman, former Rep. Henry Gonzalez, there are detention camps in America. He said that, in the name of stopping terrorism, the President could evoke the military and arrest American citizens and put them in these camps.[37]

If American troops are unwilling or unable to carry out such arrests, then the President can use Canadian troops, thanks to a military agreement called the Civil Assistance Plan.[38] The President can also use troops from the United Nations.[39]

In 2009, a bill in Congress (H.R. 645) required the Department of Homeland Security to establish at least six more detention camps on military installations. It also appears to further expand the president's emergency power.[40] Jerome Corsi observes:

> We are talking about a slippery slope: camps being prepared to be used in emergencies can easily be used to imprison dissenters.[41]

58

The bill failed to pass. However, it was introduced again on January 23, 2013 as H.R. 390. It failed to pass, but I suspect they will try again. Also it might be possible to bypass Congress and do it by means of an executive order.

Further Increasing Federal Power

The Obama administration's Financial Reform Bill was signed into law on July 21, 2010. It establishes an Office of Financial Research which would have "unprecedented, real time access to a wealth of personal and corporate financial data."[42] This new agency would not be accountable to anyone, and it could use coercion to get information.[43]

The Senate has a bill, which would give the federal government much more control over our food supply. It threatens to increase food prices and drive many small local suppliers out of business.[44] Even without this new law, Federal agents have already harassed small farms. In April 2010, they invaded a private dairy that doesn't sell to the public.[45]

The Federal Trade Commission and the Federal Communications Commission are discussing ways to regulate what Americans are able to read and hear. These proposed regulations "would apply across the board to print media, radio and television, and the internet."[46]

In July 2, 2008, presidential candidate Obama said that the military is not sufficient for our national security. He stated:

> We've got to have a civilian national security force that's
> just as powerful, just as strong, just as well funded.[47]

In March 2009, President Obama again discussed the need for a Civilian National Security Force.[48]

One approach to this is via Obama's Health Care law. It establishes a Ready Reserve Corps that would be subject to "involuntary calls to active duty during national emergencies and public health crises."[49] An article giving details about this corps is titled "Obama Just Got His Private Army."[50]

Another approach is the Universal National Service Act. If passed, this bill would require every American (including young mothers) from ages 18 to 42 to spend two years either serving in the military or doing national service as defined by the President.[51] The bill contains some provisions that could be used to promote a globalist agenda.[52]

A National Security Letter (NSL) enables the FBI and other federal agencies to require people to give them information without "probable cause" or judicial oversight. Under the Patriot Act, the NSL includes a "gag order."[53] According to Judge Andrew Napolitano, this makes it a crime for people to speak the truth. He said:

> If an FBI agent shows up at your house with a self-written search warrant, the agent will tell you, you may not tell anyone about this.[54]

According to Judge Napolitano, if a person whose home was searched in this way was questioned in court about it, under oath, he would not be able to answer truthfully without violating the Patriot Act. In other words, he would have to either commit perjury or else violate the Patriot Act.

Bypassing Congress and Ruling by Executive Regulations

On December 23rd, 2010, the Department of Interior issued a Secretarial Order giving itself the authority to designate public lands as "Wild Lands." On the same day, the Environmental Protection Agency announced it will impose carbon emission regulations on power plants and oil refineries. This is "another power grab effectively enacting what Congress had firmly rejected when presented as cap and trade legislation."[55]

The Washington Post wrote an article about these executive power grabs. It said:

The move . . . demonstrated that the Obama administration is prepared to push its environmental agenda through regulation where it has failed on Capitol Hill.[56]

Accuracy in Media called *The Washington Post's* article "matter of fact reporting about lawlessness by the federal government." It called this a reflection of the sad state of American journalism, saying:

There was no hint that this approach is illegal or unconstitutional. The account simply assumes that the Obama Administration can do what it wants, no matter what Congress or the law says.[57]

These administrative power grabs reflect the advice given in a recent report written by the Center for American Progress, which is funded by George Soros. The report is titled "The Power of the President: Recommendations to Advance Progressive Change."[58]

The original health care bill contained mandatory end-of-life counseling. Many saw this as being a slippery slope that could lead to "death panels." Because of the controversy, Congress removed the provision from the bill. But now end-of-life counseling has crept back in through a new Medicare regulation.[59] Once again, the Obama administration has used regulatory fiat to bypass the will of Congress and the American people. Charles Krauthammer said:

These regulatory power plays make political sense . . . How better to impose a liberal agenda on a center-right nation than regulatory stealth?[60]

Increasing Militarization of the Police

Police used to be "peace officers" who served and protected the public. While many devoted police officers still feel this way, the new trend is to become increasingly militarized, including using SWAT teams for minor offenses and traumatizing families in the process. For example, in 2008, a SWAT team with semi-automatic rifles raided a rural home and food co-op, holding the family (including small children) at gunpoint for hours.[61]

These days, some police officers dress and act like soldiers, complete with military-looking vehicles. You can read about the extent of what is going on and how this trend developed, in Radley Balko's book *Rise of the Warrior Cop: The Militarization of America's Police Forces*, which was published in July 2013.

> Woe unto them that call evil good, and good evil; that put darkness for light, and light for darkness; that put bitter for sweet, and sweet for bitter! Woe unto them that are wise in their own eyes, and prudent in their own sight! (Isaiah 5:20-21)

7

MAINSTREAMING OCCULTISM

Our nation is inundated with occultism, from cute little Smurfs doing magic in children's cartoons to overtly evil occultists in adult movies. Paganism and occultism (which often go together) seem to be everywhere. They are in popular music, books, movies, TV shows, and video games. They are openly endorsed on T-shirts and tattoos, in jewelry, in sculptures and pictures, and on bumper stickers.

Many people are fascinated with vampires and zombies and werewolves. There are popular romance novels and movies about normal humans falling in love with such things. One example is the *Twilight* books and movies, where girls swoon over a handsome vampire.

There is also a fascination with death. One form is "death metal" rock music and the popularity of skulls and other signs of death on clothing and even in tattoos. A more extreme form of attraction to death is when people like to spend the night at cemeteries, hoping to encounter spirits of the dead.

Such things remind me of a warning that God gave us in the Book of Proverbs:

But he that sinneth against me wrongeth his own soul:
all they that hate me love death. (Proverbs 8:36)

Ancient pagan religions are being revived. There are neo-pagans and modern druids. The Norse god Thor is being worshiped again, and people wear Thor's hammer on chains around their necks, similar to the way that Christians wear crosses. The old Celtic gods and goddesses are being worshiped again, as are ancient Greek and Roman and Babylonian deities.

Witchcraft

In our postmodern world, witchcraft has become so mainstream it is being taught in universities and nursing schools. Practical witchcraft is also being taught to young children in some of our public schools.

Witchcraft has gotten into some mainline churches. Some female ministers are also practicing witches at the same time. Two clergywomen who went through a witchcraft initiation ritual were so enthusiastic about their experience they wrote an article praising it in a publication for clergywomen. Their bishop (a woman) had attended many such rituals, which means she approves of them.[1]

Appendix A ("Goddess Worship in America") has some eye-opening information about such things, and it is all thoroughly documented.

In America, Wicca is a tax-exempt religion. It is based on witchcraft, goddess worship, and nature worship. We have Wiccan chaplains in many prisons. One such chaplain calls herself Rev. Witch.

The soap opera "Charmed" was about three sisters who were good witches. It was so popular that for years people watched the current episodes in the afternoon, and reruns of old episodes in the evening. I learned about this when I was in the hospital, because my roommate was a fan of the show. Although she called herself a

64

Christian, while she was watching one show I heard her say to herself, "I wonder if I have powers."

Sorcery

Somehow "wizard" sounds nicer than "sorcerer," doesn't it? But it's the same thing. In the old days, they were also called alchemists or those who "practice magic arts."

Sorcery used to be done in secret by men who hid what they were doing. However, thanks to the popularity of Harry Potter, people have become far more open about it.

When the first Harry Potter movie came out, I searched the Internet for things relating to Hogwarts (his school for wizards). Many of the websites were just entertainment, but some of them featured real live sorcerers who gave practical instructions in sorcery to people who came to those sites.

God Forbids Occultism

Thanks to popular books and movies, many people today believe there is "white witchcraft" which is done by "good" witches—as opposed to the bad witches. And they also believe there are "good" wizards (sorcerers).

However, that is not what God says in His Word. God makes it very clear that any kind of occultism is absolutely wrong. He calls it an abomination:

> There shall not be found among you any one that maketh his son or his daughter to pass through the fire [child sacrifice], or that useth divination [fortune telling], or an observer of times [astrology], or an enchanter [working spells], or a witch [practicing witchcraft or consulting a witch], or a charmer [using charms, amulets and other objects for protection or "good luck"], or a consulter with familiar spirits [channeling, or using Ouija boards], or a wizard [doing magic], or a necromancer [spiritism,

contacting the dead]. For all that do these things are an abomination unto the Lord. (Deuteronomy 18:10-12)

Many people think that using Ouija boards is just a game. However, if it "works," then that means they have made contact with a spirit.

Satanism

When it comes to overt evil and blasphemy, satanism is the ultimate. In spite of that, in America, it is a tax-exempt religion recognized by the state.

A friend of mine who served in the Air Force had a commanding officer who was openly a satanist. My friend told me that satanists are attracted to the military because satanism is a protected religion there. In addition, satanists can rise in the ranks and get power over other people, and they like to have power.

Some satanists are trying to change their image. For example, a satanist "church" in Oklahoma City rented out the civic center to do a "blasphemy ritual" open to the public. This particular ritual was described as being a "parody of the Catholic rite of exorcism." The purpose of the ritual was to cast out God. In other words, they openly hate God and they want to get rid of Him.

This event was advertised, and the group was interviewed by ABC News. The satanic "church" sold tickets to the event.

This satanist group claims to be benign and to have replaced devil worship with "a religion where god doesn't exist but rituals are used to empower the believer." Their leader said, "We don't kill animals, we don't kill children."[2]

If God doesn't exist, then why would they do an "exorcism" to try to cast Him out? They don't want Him to exist. But He does. And at some level they must know it.

Another attempt to mainstream satanism was to have a Black Mass at Harvard University. The local Catholics protested so much that the ritual was held off campus instead of being done at Harvard.

However, since it had received a lot of publicity, I suspect some Harvard students and local people attended, if only out of curiosity.[3]

In describing this event, *Reuters* called it a "parody" of the Catholic Mass. That term is misleading. This is not just mocking Catholicism. It is a serious attempt to blaspheme God. The satanists desecrate bread that has been consecrated by a priest. This can be accomplished in two ways. The most common is to steal consecrated hosts from a Catholic Church. But the preferred way is to have an ordained Catholic or Orthodox priest who is also a satanist.

Catholics believe that Jesus Christ is literally present in the consecrated bread and wine. Satanists also believe this, which is why they desecrate the bread and wine. They are trying to hurt and humiliate the Lord Jesus Christ.

Protestants don't believe that doctrine. Therefore, they don't believe Jesus Christ can be harmed by satanists or that He needs to be protected from them by men who are loyal to Him.

That issue is beyond the scope of this book. My point is to show the intention of the satanists. The Black Mass is a way of unleashing their hatred for God and trying to cause Him as much suffering as possible.

On September 21st, 2014, a Black Mass was held at the Oklahoma Civic Center. It was given official approval by the city officials. Tickets were sold for the event so that the public could attend it.[4]

Since two very public Black Masses have been held within several months, I would not be surprised if this becomes a trend. We could see more and more openly held satanic rituals.

This reminds me of an old poem which was written by Alexander Pope (1688-1744). The word "mein" in the poem is an old-fashioned word meaning "appearance" or "demeanor."

> Sin is a monster of such awful mein
> That to be hated needs but to be seen.
> But seen too oft, familiar of face,
> We first endure, then pity, then embrace.

There is another significant attempt to mainstream satanism. The Satanic Temple from New York is trying to force Oklahoma to allow them to put a satanic statue in Oklahoma's State Capitol. This statue will be seven feet tall so that group must have a lot of money.

Some of the height of the statue comes from a throne the devil is sitting on. The back part of the throne features a huge pentagram above the devil's head. The devil has big horns, but because they are in front of the throne, they don't stand out. Because of the throne, you don't see the shape of horns sticking up in the air by themselves.

This statue tries to make the devil look benign. He has a goat's head with horns, but his face isn't nasty. They have softened it. He is sitting on a throne that has a large pentagram, but the pentagram isn't part of him. His bat's wings look softer than demonic pictures normally do. He is modest, as his body is covered by draped cloth.

There is a little girl on one side of him and a little boy on the other side of him. The boy seems to be smiling. The devil's lap is about waist high for the sculptured children, so real live children would be able to climb up into his lap and sit there.[5]

The article about this mentions that this is a portrayal of Satan as Baphomet. However, it fails to mention this is very different from the usual statues or drawings of Baphomet intended for the use of fellow occultists. That one is naked, with the large breasts of a woman. He has a thick pentagram on his forehead. And he has a large phallus sticking up, with two snakes twined around it.

You can find pictures of Baphomet by searching for his name online. However, if you are a visual person, I don't recommend doing it because it's better not to have seriously evil images get into our heads. Personally, I wish I had never seen this thing because its face is so evil.

The statue they are trying to put in Oklahoma is an attempt to make something horribly evil appear to be harmless. And to make it appealing to children. One article about this said that the statue is intended to be "interactive with children."

Earlier I mentioned the satanic group that rented out the civic center in Oklahoma City. The group's leader said they don't kill animals or children. Well, maybe that group doesn't. Whether or not he was telling the truth, there definitely are satanic groups who kill children and animals.

I have a Christian friend who used to be a satanist. According to him, satanists kill animals during their rituals. And some satanists kill people.

I have another Christian friend who is a psychiatric nurse. She has worked with many patients who were victims of satanic ritual abuse. Many of them were raped. Some of them were forced to watch people be murdered as blood sacrifices to the devil. And some of them went through other kinds of horrible experiences.

There is an important book about this kind of thing. It tells about nation-wide child trafficking, satanic ritual murder, and political corruption at high levels, including within the FBI. The book is titled *The Franklin Cover-up: Child Abuse, Satanism, and Murder in Nebraska*. The author is John W. DeCamp, an attorney who has represented some of the victims. I'm grateful that the book exists, but I don't recommend reading it unless you have a "need to know." Some things are so evil it is better not to get them into our heads.

This stuff is for real. But the public relations arm of the satanists is trying to lure people into thinking that satanism is benign and misunderstood. They make satanism appear to be moderate and reasonable—a matter of symbols and pageantry and the empowerment of man, rather than worship of the devil. However, when listening to them, we need to remember they serve the father of lies. Jesus said:

> Ye are of your father the devil, and the lusts of your father ye will do. He was a murderer from the beginning, and abode not in the truth, because there is no truth in him. When he speaketh a lie, he speaketh of his own: for he is a liar, and the father of it. (John 8:44)

Therefore, why should we believe anything that satanists say? They are openly serving the father of lies.

Smooth-talking satanists can make it look reasonable, benign, and fascinating. And then when people are drawn to it, the satanists can spot the individuals who are ready to go "deeper" (i.e., become more overtly evil) and draw then into an inside group that does things the other people aren't aware of.

People's attitudes and beliefs vary widely. Therefore, I would expect to find "denominations" among satanists, just as there are among Christians. And even within those "denominations," there could be a wide variety of beliefs and practices, just as there are within Christian denominations. For example, the Presbyterian Church USA has voted to accept homosexual marriage. But some smaller, more conservative Presbyterian groups refuse to accept it.

Such variety can even be found within individual churches. For example, I used to attend a Baptist church whose pastor described himself as being "conservative but not fundamentalist." However, over a period of time, we came to realize he allowed serious heresies to be taught in his church. In addition, some of his sermons suggested that people should be open to such teachings. But he did it in a way that sounded learned and reasonable.

My Bible study group consisted of older people who really believed the Bible. But in that same church, there was a study group that took the teachings of the book *The Shack* very seriously. Instead of refuting it, they embraced it. *The Shack* portrays God as being a woman. It also denies sin and the need for repentance. It portrays God as having a mushy kind of love that makes no demands on His followers.[6]

The Bible calls such teaching "doctrines of devils" (1 Timothy 4:1). But the Baptist pastor who had described himself as being "conservative" defended that book when we confronted him about it, and he also promoted the book in the church's newsletter.

So within the same church there was a wide variety of people. Some were faithful Christians who believed the Bible, studied it carefully, and took God seriously. Others did not really believe the Bible, and they were wide open to any strange teachings that came along. The Bible tells us not to be "children, tossed to and fro, and carried about with every wind of doctrine, by the sleight of men, and cunning craftiness, whereby they lie in wait to deceive" (Ephesians 4:14). And it warns us:

> For the time will come when they will not endure sound doctrine; but after their own lusts shall they heap to themselves teachers, having itching ears; And they shall turn away their ears from the truth, and shall be turned unto fables. (2 Timothy 4:3-4)

We are living in times when "unthinkable" things are happening in the world and in the church. Some men who call themselves Christian pastors are actually atheists. There are so many of them they have an online support group that helps them "move beyond faith."[7]

If Christian churches can have such a wide variety of teachings, then why couldn't satanists also have a wide variety of teachings?

In addition, a "liberal" or "moderate" satanist group could be used as a recruiting ground for identifying people who have the potential to become more hard core. Such people could be invited to participate in things that are "deeper" (i.e., more overtly evil). They would become part of an inner circle that the uninitiated were not aware of.

This could be an incremental process, bringing them into deeper and deeper depravity, but doing it one small step at a time, so the people don't recognize the degree of change occurring. Incrementalism has proven to be very effective at gradually turning people into communists. As a result, somebody could start out with satanism because it seems to be hip and cool, and his favorite musician or Hollywood actor does it. And

> we are living in times when "unthinkable" things are happening in the world and in the church. Some men who call themselves Christian pastors are actually atheists

then he could wind up taking the devil more and more seriously and participating in rituals that are more and more overtly evil. And eventually he could get to the point where he does things like raping and murdering children in order to get spiritual power.

The starting point for such things can be something as simple as watching the Grammy Awards. In 2014, it featured a music video called "Dark Horse" that is overtly occult and has been described by some people as "satanic." An enthusiastic review of this music video by a popular gossip columnist referred to the two singers as being "fiery satanists." Millions of people world-wide watched the Grammy Awards, including multitudes of impressionable children. In addition, as of mid-June 2014, the online music video of "Dark Horse" had been viewed over 400 million times.[8]

What Can We Do?

In the face of such evil, we need to keep reminding ourselves that God is still on His throne. The devil is on a leash. God sets limits to what the bad guys can do. Also, God's strength is made perfect in our weakness (2 Corinthians 12:9). In addition, as Corrie ten Boom said, "If God sends us on stony paths, He provides strong shoes."

If we love God, then no matter what happens, God will use it for our long-term, eternal good. He will use it to bring us closer to Himself, to teach us to trust Him more, and to develop more godly character.

That also applies to the people we love. If they love God, then God will make everything work out for their good. But if they don't love God, then nothing will do them any good. What is the use of having a pleasant life here and then going to Hell?

Therefore, nobody is at the mercy of men or of circumstances. The bottom line is our relationship with God. Do we love Him?

**Jesus said unto him, Thou shalt love the Lord
thy God with all thy heart, and with all thy
soul, and with all thy mind. (Matthew 22:37)**

8

DEALING WITH SHOCK

Yea, and all that will live godly in Christ Jesus shall suffer persecution. (2 Timothy 3:12)

Persecution is shocking. It's cruel and unfair. Why do people punish us for doing good? Why do they hate us for loving Jesus? It just doesn't make sense. It seems crazy.

It certainly doesn't make sense to reasonable people who know God and have a biblical standard of right and wrong. In contrast, the devil's values are upside down, and he is literally insane. He had to be, in order to think he could fight against God *and win*.

As Christians serve God, they increasingly see things from His perspective. Those who serve the devil (whether knowingly or unknowingly) wind up thinking more and more the way he does.

Many people blame God when cruel and unjust things are done to them. But they are accusing the wrong person. They should be blaming Adam and Eve instead of God. Everything bad that happens to us is because Adam and Eve rebelled against God in the Garden of Eden.

Try to put yourself in God's shoes for a moment. He created a perfect world in which everything was good. Adam and Eve were created as mature adults, ready for marriage. They never had a troubled childhood. They didn't have any old wounds or scars. They had a closeness to God we can't begin to comprehend, walking and talking with Him every evening. Their world was beautiful and safe. They were healthy and had wonderful things to eat all around them, waiting to be picked and enjoyed. All of their needs were met, and all of their desires were fulfilled.

Then along came the serpent, who was the world's first con artist. He talked them into rebelling against God.

When everything was perfect, both Adam and Eve fell into sin. That is a hundred percent rate of failure. Now, if having everything be perfect doesn't work, then what is the only alternative? Suffering. Hardship. Death. Discovering we desperately need God.

My mom wrote a poem about the shock and challenge of having normal life suddenly be radically changed in painful and confusing ways:

TRUST
(by Frances Morrisson)

**Suddenly the Everyday
is wrenched away.**

**Lord, please guard and grow
the fullness of my love and trust in You.
When all I know is set afloat today,
pilot my boat and nudge me to
the harbor of the Narrow Way**

**There let me find a clearer, newer view
where all that's upside down
resolves; makes sense; steady in the
light of love and Trust in You.**

"Wrenched away" is a good description of what persecution feels like. This applies to a Christian baker who has been threatened with prison because he refused to bake a wedding cake for a homosexual marriage,[1] and it also applies to a Christian in the Middle East who is beheaded because of his faith. It's shocking, and something inside us cries out, "This can't be happening!" There is distress and grief, pain and confusion.

Obviously, what the baker suffered is not as serious as being beheaded, but it's still a shock. There is a difference in the degree of severity of the persecution, but it's a gut-wrenching event for the people involved in both situations. Comparing it to animals, it is better to be attacked by an angry bobcat than by a man-eating tiger. However, either way, there is a lot of suffering involved.

The best antidote for shock, pain, and suffering is the Word of God. It is also the best guide for how to respond to the challenges of life. Therefore, I am going to quote a lot of Scripture in this chapter.

The Bible tells us that Christians should expect to be persecuted. However, until recently, American Christians were usually treated well. This feels normal for us, but it is unusual in terms of the world today since many countries have serious persecution. Now Christians in the United States (and Canada too) are suffering for their faith. For Americans, this is shocking, but according to the Bible, we should not be surprised:

> And he said to them all, If any man will come after me, let him deny himself, and take up his cross daily, and follow me. (Luke 9:23)

> Yea, and all that will live godly in Christ Jesus shall suffer persecution. (2 Timothy 3:12)

> Remember the word that I said unto you. The servant is not greater than his lord. If they have persecuted me, they will also persecute you; if they have kept my saying, they will keep yours also. (John 15:20)

> We are troubled on every side, yet not distressed; we are perplexed, but not in despair; Persecuted, but not forsaken; cast down, but not destroyed. (2 Corinthians 4:8-9)

> Who shall separate us from the love of Christ? Shall tribulation, or distress, or persecution, or famine, or nakedness, or peril, or sword? As it is written, For thy sake we are killed all the day long; we are accounted as sheep for the slaughter. Nay, in all these things we are more than conquerors through him that loved us. (Romans 8:35-37)

The good news is that God enables His people to endure persecution. His grace is sufficient to get us through the trials and tribulations, and if we love Him and put our trust in Him, then He will make whatever we go through work out for our good:

> These things I have spoken unto you, that in me ye might have peace. In the world ye shall have tribulation: but be of good cheer; I have overcome the world. (John 16:33)

> And we know that all things work together for good to them that love God, to them who are the called according to his purpose. (Romans 8:28)

According to the Bible, God uses trials and tribulations to build godly character in us. This is good fruit in our lives, and it will be a blessing for us and for others. The suffering is temporary, but the rewards will be eternal:

> Beloved, think it not strange concerning the fiery trial which is to try you, as though some strange thing happened unto you: But rejoice, inasmuch as ye are partakers of Christ's sufferings; that, when his glory shall be revealed, ye may be glad also with exceeding joy. If ye be reproached for the name of Christ, happy are ye; for the spirit of glory and of God resteth upon you: on their part he is evil spoken of, but on your part he is glorified. (1 Peter 4:12-14)

My brethren, count it all joy when ye fall into divers temptations; Knowing this, that the trying of your faith worketh patience. But let patience have her perfect work, that ye may be perfect and entire, wanting nothing. (James 1:2-4)

[W]e glory in tribulations also: knowing that tribulation worketh patience; And patience, experience; and experience, hope. (Romans 5:3-4)

Jesus told us it is a blessing to be persecuted for His sake. Now in terms of my emotions, I have real difficulty with that. I want to avoid suffering, and it pains me to see others suffer. However, God sees the big picture. I don't. God knows what He is talking about.

My perspective is limited by my natural fears. Therefore, I need to take God at His word and believe Him, in spite of the fact that what He says goes against the grain. Here is what Jesus said:

Blessed are they which are persecuted for righteousness' sake: for theirs is the kingdom of heaven. (Matthew 5:10)

Blessed are ye, when men shall revile you, and persecute you, and shall say all manner of evil against you falsely, for my sake. Rejoice, and be exceeding glad: for great is your reward in heaven: for so persecuted they the prophets which were before you. (Matthew 5:11-12)

I am not at the point of being able to "rejoice" or be "exceeding glad" if I am persecuted, or if people I know and love are persecuted. However, I can tell God, "This does not feel like a blessing to me, but You say that it is a blessing. Please change my heart, and enable me to see it the way that You see it."

There is a story about a little boy who was with his father during a terrorist attack. There was gunfire, shouting, and confusion. When it was all over, the father asked his son, "Were you afraid?" And his boy answered, "No, Daddy. You were holding my hand."

That's the way we need to be with the Lord.

God is faithful. He loves us. He promises He will always be with us. And He knows what He is doing. He sees the really big picture. We can't comprehend it yet.

GOD'S LOVE
(by Maria Kneas)

The God who made the earth
Has always loved us.
Before we drew a breath,
Our heart was known.
God created us
To live with Him forever,
To sing and dance
With joy before His throne.

Our time on earth is hard,
But it is fleeting.
No matter how things seem,
God's always there.
He'll guide us and protect us
And watch over us,
And take away each tear and fear and care.

And when the toil and pain
And fear have ended,
When sorrow's gone,
And all we know is love,
Then we and God
Will celebrate forever,
Rejoicing with the saints in Heaven above.

9

FIGHTING FEAR

And the Lord, he it is that doth go before
thee; he will be with thee, he will not fail
thee, neither forsake thee: fear not, neither
be dismayed. (Deuteronomy 31:8)

I know something about fighting fear because I've had a problem
with fear all of my life. My dad was sent home from World War
II in a hospital ship after attempting suicide, and my Mom was
always afraid he would try it again.

Fear is contagious. Children pick up what their parents are feeling. Every night, I had a nightmare about being chased by something
horrible, but I didn't know what it was.

When I was fifteen years old, Mom told me to let Dad know
that dinner was ready. I found him lying in bed, unconscious from
an attempt to commit suicide. Mercifully, we discovered him soon
enough, and he recovered at the hospital.

I married a strong, healthy young man, and three years into our
marriage, he had a massive heart attack. He needed a quadruple bypass
but wasn't strong enough to get the surgery because of the damage done
to his heart. After a year of living with painful and debilitating heart
problems, he died. During that year, every day when I was at work, I
never knew if I would find him dead on the floor when I came home.

There have been other fearful things in my life, including cancer. The point is, even without persecution, we have to deal with fear. Drastic things can happen suddenly, without warning.

I had to overcome some fear in order to write this book, because the people who hate Christianity will not appreciate having this book be published. Some of those people work in our government. According to official government documents, I would be classified as an "extremist" and a "potential terrorist" because I am an evangelical Christian; I take what the Bible says about the end times seriously, and I believe that unborn babies should not be killed.[1]

The Bible says love is an antidote to fear. Therefore, anything we can do to increase our love for God and for one another will help get rid of fear. The Bible says:

> There is no fear in love; but perfect love casteth out fear: because fear hath torment. He that feareth is not made perfect in love. (1 John 4:18)

Our natural human love is inadequate. However, we can ask the Lord to give us His love, to enable us to love the way He does. The Bible says He can do that:

> And hope maketh not ashamed; because *the love of God is shed abroad in our hearts by the Holy Ghost* which is given unto us. (Romans 5:5, emphasis added)

God can enable us to do things we would never be able to do in our own strength. We are weak, but He is strong. And He is faithful to help His own. The Bible says:

> I can do all things through Christ which strengtheneth me. (Philippians 4:13)

The Lord is my light and my salvation; whom shall I fear? the Lord is the strength of my life; of whom shall I be afraid? (Psalm 27:1)

My flesh and my heart faileth: but God is the strength of my heart, and my portion for ever. (Psalm 73:26)

A good antidote to the fear of what men can do to us is the "fear of the Lord." This involves more than just reverence. It also includes the fear of God's punishment. If our love isn't strong enough to enable us to do what is right, then the fear of the Lord can give us the strength to do it.

According to the Bible, the fear of the Lord also gives us wisdom and understanding. It enables us to be rightly related to God.

It's good when we can do the right thing because we love God. But when we are unable to do that, then we can recognize God's power and authority, salute Him, and say, "Yes, Sir!"

After my dad became a Christian, he used to talk about the importance of "taking God seriously." That includes the fear of the Lord. The Bible talks about how important it is:

The fear of the Lord is the beginning of wisdom: and the knowledge of the holy is understanding. (Proverbs 9:10)

Behold, the eye of the Lord is upon them that fear him, upon them that hope in his mercy. (Psalm 33:18)

The angel of the Lord encampeth round about them that fear him, and delivereth them. (Psalm 34:7)

There is a song based on that last Scripture about the angel of the Lord protecting those who fear Him. One night I had to walk through a dangerous neighborhood, and I was afraid. As I walked, I quietly sang that song. I started out feeling afraid, but as I kept singing, the fear decreased. And God protected me.

Another antidote to fear is keeping the big picture in mind—eternity. This world is not really our home. We are citizens of the kingdom of God. Our true home is Heaven, and our true king is Almighty God.

The apostle Paul said we are "ambassadors" for Jesus Christ:

> Now then we are ambassadors for Christ. (2 Corinthians 5:20)

Think about what it means to be an ambassador. You have to leave your native land and live in another country, surrounded by people whose customs and values are different from yours. They may even be cruel and barbaric. (Can you imagine what it would be like to be an ambassador in a place like North Korea or Saudi Arabia?) You are only there temporarily, representing the government of your own country. At some point, your ruler will call you back to your native land.

The book *Pilgrim's Progress* by John Bunyan describes us as being pilgrims on a journey through this world, on our way to Heaven. An old spiritual hymn has the same theme. Sometimes I sing this song when I read distressing news about what is going on in the world:

POOR WAYFARING STRANGER
(19th century)

I am a poor wayfaring stranger
Traveling through this world of woe
But there's no trouble, toil or danger
In that bright land to which I go.

It helps to remember that our time here on earth is only temporary and that this world is passing away. Here are two Scripture passages that give us the eternal perspective. I often think about this. The one from the book of Revelation is one of my favorite passages in the Bible:

> And God shall wipe away all tears from their eyes; and there shall be no more death, neither sorrow, nor crying,

neither shall there be any more pain: for the former things are passed away. And he that sat upon the throne said, Behold, I make all things new. (Revelation 21:4 5)

Sometimes worship can dispel fear. About twenty years ago, a mammogram showed signs of possible cancer in both of my breasts, and I had to get a biopsy done. I asked my surgeon to use a local anesthesia, because that is less stressful to the body, and he agreed to do so. I wound up with two doctors cutting on me at the same time (one working on each breast). Evidently, they forgot I was awake, because they were talking about seeing things that looked like cancer.

That was a frightening situation. The more they talked, the greater my fear became. Then I remembered a Scripture passage:

I will bless the Lord at all times: his praise shall continually be in my mouth. (Psalm 34:1)

They were playing music in the operating room. I asked them to turn it off, which they did. Then I began to sing a worship song based on Scripture. By the time I finished singing the first line of that song, the fear just drained away.

All during that procedure, I kept on singing. One of the nurses knew the songs, and she sang along with me. I was at peace, focused on God instead of my ailing body. I was thinking about God's love and faithfulness, instead of worrying about my future. (As a result of that biopsy, I had a double radical mastectomy, followed by chemotherapy. The hardships I went through brought me closer to God. Being faced with your mortality changes your priorities, and it makes you know that you need God.)

No matter what happens to us, God is always worthy of our praise. The Bible says:

O magnify the Lord with me, and let us exalt his name together. (Psalm 34:3)

When we "magnify" the Lord, we don't make Him bigger. He is already much greater than we can possibly comprehend. What we do is make ourselves more capable of recognizing His greatness. When we do that, God seems larger to us, which makes our problems seem smaller by comparison. Here are some Scriptures that remind us of how great and mighty our God is:

> Thus saith the Lord, The heaven is my throne, and the earth is my footstool. (Isaiah 66:1)

> I am God, and there is none else; I am God, and there is none like me, Declaring the end from the beginning, and from ancient times the things that are not yet done, saying, My counsel shall stand, and I will do all my pleasure. (Isaiah 46:9-10)

> The heavens declare the glory of God; and the firmament sheweth his handywork. (Psalm 19:1)

One thing that can cause fear is sins we have not dealt with. That puts a barrier between us and God, which makes it more difficult for us to turn to Him and to trust Him. Therefore, it is good to habitually invite God to search our hearts and show us if there is anything we need to repent of. King David said:

> Who can understand his errors? cleanse thou me from secret faults. Keep back thy servant also from presumptuous sins; let them not have dominion over me: then shall I be upright, and I shall be innocent from the great transgression. Let the words of my mouth, and the meditation of my heart, be acceptable in thy sight, O Lord, my strength, and my redeemer. (Psalm 19:12-14)

> Create in me a clean heart, O God; and renew a right spirit within me. (Psalm 51:10)

America has become a sex-saturated society. As a result, much of our entertainment contains things intended to incite lust. So do many commercials. Jesus warned us:

> But I say unto you, That whosoever looketh on a woman to lust after her hath committed adultery with her already in his heart. (Matthew 5:28)

Obviously, that principle applies to women as well as to men. Our society takes such things lightly, but God takes them very seriously:

> Now the works of the flesh are manifest, which are these; Adultery, fornication, uncleanness, lasciviousness [lustful], Idolatry, witchcraft, hatred, variance [contentions], emulations [jealousy], wrath, strife, seditions, heresies, Envyings, murders, drunkenness, revellings, and such like: of the which I tell you before, as I have also told you in time past, that they which do such things shall not inherit the kingdom of God. (Galatians 5:19-21)

Obviously, nobody is going to be perfect this side of Heaven. We will keep falling into sin. The point is, when we sin, are we distressed about it? Do we repent? Do we make a serious effort to stop doing it? Do we keep asking God to help us overcome it? Are we doing it more and more, and getting hardened to it? Or are we doing it less and less? What direction are we moving in?

When it comes to repenting for sins, abortion can be a real stumbling block, because the world keeps telling us that what a pregnant woman has inside her is not a baby. The problem is, how can you repent for something you think is not a sin?

This is a strange double standard, because the world will put Americans in jail for destroying an eagle's egg. They know there is a baby eagle in there. Everybody knows that a pregnant cat has kittens inside her, and a pregnant dog has puppies inside her.

The world tells us that what a pregnant woman has inside her is only a "fetus." Well, the word "fetus" is just a Latin word that means "child." Doctors like using Latin terms for things.

There are many photos of babies in the womb who are sucking their thumbs. They are obviously babies and not blobs of tissue. Even sonograms can be clear enough to show that.

The Bible makes it obvious that what a woman carries inside her is a baby. In the Gospel of Luke, we are told that Mary became pregnant supernaturally when the Holy Spirit came upon her. Then she went to visit her cousin Elizabeth, who was six months pregnant with John the Baptist.

As soon as Mary walked into the room, carrying her recently conceived baby in her womb, the baby inside Elizabeth's womb recognized Jesus and leaped for joy. We are also told that John the Baptist was filled with the Holy Spirit while he was still inside his mother's womb:

> And it came to pass, that, when Elisabeth heard the salutation of Mary, the babe leaped in her womb; and *Elisabeth was filled with the Holy Ghost*: And she spake out with a loud voice, and said, Blessed art thou among women, and blessed is the fruit of thy womb. And whence is this to me, that the mother of my Lord should come to me? For, lo, *as soon as the voice of thy salutation sounded in mine ears, the babe leaped in my womb for joy.* (Luke 1:41-44, emphasis added)

> For he shall be great in the sight of the Lord, and shall drink neither wine nor strong drink; *and he shall be filled with the Holy Ghost, even from his mother's womb.* (Luke 1:15, emphasis added)

God can call a person to ministry before they are born. We see this with the prophet Jeremiah. God told him:

> Before I formed thee in the belly I knew thee; and before
> thou camest forth out of the womb I sanctified thee, and I
> ordained thee a prophet unto the nations. (Jeremiah 1:5)

If you have had an abortion or have encouraged anybody else to have one, then please repent. God will forgive you. He loves you.

You might find it helpful to read Psalm 51. David wrote it after the prophet Nathan confronted him about committing adultery with Bathsheba and setting up her husband Uriah to be killed, which in essence was murdering him. The Bible says that David had a heart for God, and he repented (1 Kings 11:4). In the Gospels, Jesus is called the "son of David" (Matthew 9:27, 15:22; Mark 10:47-48).

One thing that can cause fear is the fact that occultism is becoming mainstream. Satanists and witches desire to put spells and curses on Christians. In case you think such things are not real, the Bible says they are:

> And Moses and Aaron went in unto Pharaoh, and they
> did so as the Lord had commanded: and Aaron cast down
> his rod before Pharaoh, and before his servants, and it
> became a serpent. Then Pharaoh also called the wise men
> and the sorcerers: now the magicians of Egypt, they also
> did in like manner with their enchantments. For they cast
> down every man his rod, and they became serpents: but
> Aaron's rod swallowed up their rods. (Exodus 7:10-12)

Notice that Aaron did something supernatural in the power of God, and then Pharoah's sorcerers did the same kind of thing, using "enchantments" (spells). However, Pharoah's sorcerers were not able to harm Moses or Aaron, because Aaron's serpent ate ("swallowed") the serpents of the sorcerers.

The bad news is that occult power is very real. The good news is that God is infinitely greater, and He takes care of His own. He is willing and able to protect us.

When you drive down a country road, you can go off that road on either side and wind up in a ditch. When it comes to the occult, we can fall into two ditches.

One ditch is to deny the existence and power of the devil and his demons. This means denying the Bible, because Jesus is often shown casting out demons. And according to Mark 16:17, Jesus gave those who believe in Him the power to cast out demons. We see a number of examples of this in the Book of Acts.

The other ditch is to "see a demon behind every bush," as the saying goes. Here's an example from my life. I'm overweight. One day I was eating a candy bar, and a woman who claimed to have a deliverance ministry tried to cast a "demon of chocolate" out of me. That kind of nonsense gives Christians a bad name.

When God confronts the devil, it is *not* like a wrestling match. It is more like squashing a bug with your finger, or flicking a fly off your shoulder. Almighty God has absolute power over the devil. God allows him to do some things, but the devil is on a leash, and eventually he will be thrown into the Lake of Fire (Revelation 20:10). Look at what Jesus said:

> But if I *with the finger of God cast out devils*, no doubt the kingdom of God is come upon you. (Luke 11:20, emphasis added)

> Behold, I give unto you power to tread on serpents and scorpions, and *over all the power of the enemy*: and nothing shall by any means hurt you. (Luke 10:19, emphasis added)

We see a physical example of this when the apostle Paul was bitten by a poisonous snake. The natives knew this snake was deadly, and they expected Paul to die, but it didn't harm him at all:

> And when Paul had gathered a bundle of sticks, and laid them on the fire, *there came a viper out of the heat, and fastened on his hand.* And when the barbarians saw

the venomous beast hang on his hand, they said among themselves, No doubt this man is a murderer, whom, though he hath escaped the sea, yet vengeance suffereth not to live. And he shook off the beast into the fire, and *felt no harm.* Howbeit they looked when he should have swollen, or fallen down dead suddenly: but after they had looked a great while, and *saw no harm come to him,* they changed their minds, and said that he was a god. (Acts 28:3-6, emphasis added)

What happened to Paul demonstrates God's protection from deadly physical things. However, the "power of the enemy" means spiritual dangers as well as physical ones. God is able to protect us from curses and spells.

God protects us. However, the Bible also tells us we should protect ourselves by putting on the "armor of God." We are to be active, not passive:

Finally, my brethren, be strong in the Lord, and in the power of his might. Put on the whole armour of God, that ye may be able to stand against the wiles of the devil. For we wrestle not against flesh and blood, but against principalities, against powers, against the rulers of the darkness of this world, against spiritual wickedness in high places. Wherefore take unto you the whole armour of God, that ye may be able to withstand in the evil day, and having done all, to stand. Stand therefore, having your loins girt about with *truth*, and having on the breastplate of *righteousness*; And your feet shod with the preparation of the gospel of peace; Above all, taking the shield of *faith*, wherewith ye shall be able to quench all the fiery darts of the wicked. And take the helmet of salvation, and the sword of the Spirit, which is the *word of God: Praying always* with all prayer and supplication in the Spirit, and watching thereunto with all perseverance and supplication for all saints. (Ephesians 6:10-18, emphasis added)

According to this passage, we are not to be passive. God expects us to love the truth, have faith, get the Word of God in us (develop a working knowledge of the Bible by reading it and studying it), and pray "always." Obviously, we can't be on our knees praying all day long, but we can have a spirit of prayer. We can be aware of God, and stay in communication with Him throughout the day.

Before my husband died, we could be in the same room, doing different things, and not talking to one another. However, we felt one another's presence. We were aware of the other person, even when we were intensely focused on something else. There was an awareness of the one we love, and it was easy to talk from time to time.

We can be the same way with God. We can have times of intense prayer, but we can also talk with Him as we go about our daily routines—when we are cooking, or walking somewhere, or driving, or eating a meal.

God has ways of communicating with us. One of them is bringing Scriptures to mind. Another is nudging us, like a sheep dog nudges the sheep to get them to go where they need to be:

> But the Comforter, which is the Holy Ghost, whom the Father will send in my name, he shall teach you all things, and bring all things to your remembrance, whatsoever I have said unto you. (John 14:26)

> My sheep hear my voice, and I know them, and they follow me. (John 10:27)

A good example of God leading us (or nudging us) is the Christian mother whose son is a soldier in Afghanistan. One night she wakes up, feeling an urgent need to pray for her boy, so she prays her heart out for him. Then several weeks later, she gets a letter from her son, saying that his unit was ambushed. Some men were killed, and others were wounded, but he was not harmed. The mother looks at the date when the ambush occurred, and she realizes it happened during the time she was praying for her boy.

For an excellent study of the armor of God, I recommend the website by Berit Kjos, *The Shepherd's Way*. Look at the section titled "The Armor of God" (www.shepherd.to).

In addition to this article, under the section titled "Bible Studies" there is a more in-depth study of this called "A Wardrobe from the King." This is a series of studies (one for each piece of the armor).

The Bible tells us to "cast" our cares (fears, anxieties, worries, and concerns) on God because He cares for us (loves us and takes good care of us). That means giving our cares to God, and leaving them with Him—not taking them back again:

> Casting all your care upon him; for he careth for you.
> (1 Peter 5:7)

This is easier said than done. We have to learn how to do it. Like many things in life, it takes practice. We can ask God to enable us to do it, to give us the grace for it, and to help us appropriate and work with the grace He gives us.

This morning, a prayer came to me. I would like to share it with you. The prayer is based on some Scripture passages, so I'll give them first:

> And *let the peace of God rule in your hearts*, to the which also ye are called in one body; and be ye thankful. (Colossians 3:15, emphasis added)

> For it is God which worketh in you both *to will* and *to do* of his good pleasure. (Philippians 2:13, emphasis added)

> O Lord, thou art our father; we are the clay, and thou our potter; and we all are the work of thy hand. (Isaiah 64:8)

> There is no fear in love; but *perfect love casteth out fear*: because fear hath torment. He that feareth is not made perfect in love. (1 John 4:18, emphasis added)

Ye are the light of the world. A city that is set on an hill cannot be hid. (Matthew 5:14, emphasis added)

Let your light so shine before men, that they may see your good works, and glorify your Father which is in heaven. (Matthew 5:16, emphasis added)

That ye may be blameless and harmless, the sons of God, without rebuke, in the midst of a crooked and perverse nation, among whom ye *shine as lights in the world.* (Philippians 2:15, emphasis added)

PRAYER: Lord, how do I let Your peace rule in my heart? You told me to do it, which means it is possible to do it, and You expect me to do it. However, I have fear and anxiety in my heart, which means that Your peace is not ruling in me. Please forgive me for not doing what You told me to do.

Lord, I don't know how to do it. Please show me how. Teach me. You are the Creator. I'm just a creature. You are my Father. I'm just a child. You are the potter. I'm just the clay. Please change me. Make me into a person who does it as a way of life.

Lord, please give me the grace to do it. Deal with anything in me that hinders Your peace, that blocks it in any way. Be glorified in my life. Fill me with Your peace and Your love in a way that gives You glory.

You said that perfect love casts out fear. But I have fear in my heart. That means I don't have enough love for You or for others. My love isn't good enough. It isn't strong enough. Please put Your love in my heart. Let Your love be shed abroad in my heart.

You told us to be lights in the darkness. Showing Your peace and Your love in the midst of trials and tribulations is one way of doing that.

I want to bear good fruit for Your Kingdom, and this fear and worry are getting in the way. Please set me free from them. In Jesus' name. Amen.

10

THE BOTTOM LINE

**[C]hoose you this day whom ye will serve
. . . but as for me and my house, we will
serve the LORD. (Joshua 24:15)**

Our human thinking is flawed, and we all have blind spots. Even pastors and seminary professors make mistakes in their thinking. That is why the Bible tells us:

Trust in the LORD with all thine heart; and lean not unto thine own understanding. In all thy ways acknowledge him, and he shall direct thy paths. (Proverbs 3:5-6)

Our understanding is valuable, but it has limitations. We are children of God. Our heavenly Father knows everything. However, since we are "children," we are limited in our comprehension. We all make mistakes. The only man who ever got everything right was the Lord Jesus Christ.

Even the apostle Paul had limitations in his understanding. He wrote nearly a fourth of the New Testament, and much of our theology is based on his writings, but he said:

> For now we see through a glass darkly; but then face to
> face: *now I know in part*; but then shall I know even as
> also I am known. (1 Corinthians 13:12, emphasis added)

Paul said he only knew "in part." He didn't fully comprehend everything. If Paul's understanding was incomplete, then modern Christians (who depend on Paul's writings) are even more limited in their understanding.

Therefore, we cannot have unquestioning confidence in any denomination, or church, or pastor, or teacher. We must test *everything* against what the Bible says. We need to do our own praying, and our own Bible studying, instead of relying on "experts" to do it for us.

Having a church and a pastor is valuable, and we should treasure them, but we need to be able to stand on our own if necessary. Even with a good church and a good pastor, we need to test everything we are taught against Scripture. Good pastors can change. Sometimes all it takes is attending one conference or reading one book. The Bible warns us:

> Cursed be the man that trusteth in man, and maketh
> flesh his arm, and whose heart departeth from the LORD.
> (Jeremiah 17:5)

When the disciples asked Jesus what the signs of His return would be, the very first thing He said was:

> Take heed that no man deceive you. (Matthew 24:4)

Today, some pastors openly deny the resurrection of Jesus Christ. My city has a large Baptist church whose pastor denies the atonement (that Jesus died to save us from our sins). Some of these heretics have large, prosperous churches, so they probably have charismatic attention-getting personalities. Their preaching sounds good to people who don't really think about what has been said or who haven't read enough of the Bible to recognize when statements are contrary to Scripture.

Some pastors don't believe in God, so many that they have an online support group. Their motto is "Moving beyond faith."[1]

The fact that such men can be pastors is amazing. Why don't the members of their churches recognize that something is seriously wrong and either get rid of those pastors or else leave those churches?

We need to be on guard, because the devil wants to undermine our faith. The Bible warns us:

> Be sober, be vigilant; because your adversary the devil, as a roaring lion, walketh about, seeking whom he may devour. (1 Peter 5:8)

Will we take a stand for true Christian doctrine, even if our family and our friends mock us because of it? And even if our pastor says we are wrong?

Will we take a stand for biblical standards of morality, even if the world calls it "hate speech"? Or if it is called a "hate crime," for which we can go to jail?

Where do our priorities lie? The Bible warns us against compromising our faith because of the fear of what men may do to us. Jesus told us not to be afraid of those who can kill our bodies, but "rather fear him which is able to destroy both soul and body in hell" (Matthew 10:28).

This is where the "fear of the Lord" becomes important. Our actions and attitudes have eternal consequences. Therefore, we need to have a healthy fear of God.

These days, it is popular to say that the "fear of the Lord" just means reverence. Well, it includes reverence, but it means more than that. God is our Judge, and He can send us to Hell. Jesus warned us that some people who think they are good Christians will wind up in Hell. He said:

Not every one that saith unto me, Lord, Lord, shall enter into the kingdom of heaven; but he that doeth the will of my Father which is in heaven. Many will say to me in that day, Lord, Lord, have we not prophesied in thy name? and in thy name have cast out devils? and in thy name done many wonderful works? And then will I profess unto them, I never knew you: depart from me, ye that work iniquity. (Matthew 7:21-23)

Jesus also warned us that following Him would result in suffering. Some people react to hardship by getting angry at God and turning away from Him. Jesus told us:

And blessed is he, whosoever shall not be offended in me. (Luke 7:23)

Sometimes people become offended with God when they don't understand what God is doing. The Bible gives us an example of that:

Many therefore of his disciples, when they had heard this, said, This is an hard saying; who can hear it? When Jesus knew in himself that his disciples murmured at it, he said unto them, Doth this offend you? . . . From that time many of his disciples went back, and walked no more with him. Then said Jesus unto the twelve, Will ye also go away? Then Simon Peter answered him, Lord, to whom shall we go? thou hast the words of eternal life. (John 6:60-61, 66-68)

Persecution is increasing. "Unthinkable" things are happening in the world today. When the pain and the sorrow come, will we turn to God? Or will we turn away from Him?

If things happen that we cannot understand, will we become offended with God?

If things turn out differently than we expected, based on what our pastor or our Sunday school teacher told us, will we say the

Bible isn't true? Will we call God a liar? Or will we say our pastor or Sunday school teacher was mistaken?

Will we be like the disciples who became offended with Jesus and "walked no more with him"? Or will we be like Peter, who stuck with Jesus in spite of everything?

That's the bottom line, and our eternal destiny depends on what we do then.

Heaven and Hell are very real. There is far more at stake than we can comprehend now. We won't fully understand it until we see Jesus face to face.

CHOOSE LIFE
(by Maria Kneas)

God sets before you life and death.
Choose life.

Jesus is the Way, the Truth and the Life.
The devil is a liar and a thief.
He wants to kill your hope and steal your joy
And fill your days with endless grief.

Jesus came to give unshakeable peace
And the only freedom that's real.
He wants to fill your heart with everlasting joy.
He wants to love and bless and heal.

God sets before you life and death.
Choose life.

THE BEST WAY TO BUILD UP
OUR FAITH IS TO OBEY GOD.
WHEN WE OBEY HIM, THEN WE
GROW IN OUR UNDERSTANDING
OF HIM, AND WE LEARN TO
TRUST HIM MORE. THAT MAKES
IT EASIER FOR US TO OBEY
HIM. IT'S A GOOD CYCLE.

11

BUILDING FAITH

But ye, beloved, *building up yourselves on your most holy faith*, praying in the Holy Ghost, Keep yourselves in the love of God, looking for the mercy of our Lord Jesus Christ unto eternal life. (Jude 1:20-21, emphasis added)

Persecution is increasing world-wide. In America, we are in the early stages of persecution, and it is getting worse. If there ever was a time to have our faith built up, it is now. Difficult times are on the increase, and for many, it will become insurmountable.

The Word

The Bible says it is impossible to please God without faith (Hebrews 11:6), and faith comes by hearing the Word of God (Romans 10:17). In order to increase faith, we need to develop a working knowledge of the Bible, because that is where God tells us what He is like and how He wants us to live. If we have a church with good, biblical preaching, that is a wonderful blessing. However, we cannot depend on our pastor. We need to know the Bible ourselves.

If persecution becomes full blown, Bibles may be outlawed, especially the more literal translations (e.g. *KJV*). Therefore, we need to get the Word of God inside us now—while we still can.

We can no longer take having Bibles or being able to go to church for granted. A time may come when even meeting with a few friends to pray and talk about Scripture will become dangerous. Jesus warned us:

> Then shall they deliver you up to be afflicted, and shall kill you: and ye shall be hated of all nations for my name's sake. And then shall many be offended, and shall betray one another, and shall hate one another. (Matthew 24:9-10)

I have friends who have been memorizing Scripture for years for that very reason. Some also memorize hymns and worship songs, so they can sing them silently in their head. That is what the Bible calls "making melody in your heart to the Lord" (Ephesians 5:19).

When we read the Bible, it is good to ask God to give us understanding. He wrote it by having the Holy Spirit show various human authors what to say and how to say it. God knows what the Scriptures mean, and He can open our eyes and our hearts to the truth in the Bible.

There are some things we can't really understand now, but God will give us the understanding if and when we need it. For example, some things in the book of Revelation will become very clear to the Christians who are alive when those events occur. They will be able to say, "Oh, so that's what God meant!"

We see an example of that in the Gospels when they say that certain events fulfilled specific prophecies. At the time the prophets wrote those prophecies, they didn't necessarily understand what it was about. Hundreds of years later, when those prophecies were fulfilled, then it became clear.

Praise and Worship

We can also build faith through praising and worshiping God. The Bible says that God "inhabits" our praise (Psalm 22:3). I don't understand that intellectually, but it implies that when we worship, there is a kind of closeness to God we don't have otherwise.

Paul said that Christ is *in* us (Colossians 1:27). You can't get any closer than that. So it may be that what worship does is to make us more aware of God's presence, to make us more sensitive to Him. We can become so preoccupied with the cares of daily life that we tune God out. Then, when we worship, we get our focus back and become more aware of Him.

Prayer

Another way to build our faith is through prayer. Again, that makes us more aware of God. It gets us tuned in to Him. It reminds us of His love and His faithfulness and how He takes care of us and those we love.

When we see answers to prayer, those answers increase our faith. However, if we don't see an answer to prayer, that should not discourage us. God may be working behind the scenes in a way we don't understand. Or it may be we are not praying according to His will, that what we want would not be good for us or for those we are praying for.

God sees the big picture. We don't. Our human understanding is very limited.

Children often ask their parents for things, which would not be good for them. For example, many young boys want to drive the family car, but the results would be disastrous because they don't have the judgment, skill, or maturity to do it safely. However, they don't understand that. When parents refuse such requests, it's because they love their children and don't want them to get hurt. Well, God is the same way with us.

One thing that can increase our love for God (which increases our faith in Him) is to go through some of the things that Jesus suffered. Paul said:

> That I may know him, and the power of his resurrection, and the fellowship of his sufferings, being made conformable unto his death. (Philippians 3:10)

For example, have you ever done something good and had people misunderstand you, criticize you for it, or even punish you for doing the right thing? If so, then that will give you some understanding of what Jesus went through His entire life. When He healed people out of love and compassion, the Pharisees wanted to kill Him because of it. Eventually, they were able to have Him crucified.

What we suffer is small compared to what Jesus endured, but it can help us know Him better and love Him more. It gives us more reasons to be grateful to Him, because it gives us some understanding of how much He was willing to go through in order to save us.

Study Scripture and Beware of the Skeptics

Christians need to stand firm for what we believe in rather than allow everything we stand for to be progressively eroded. And to do this we need to be quite sure of what we believe, quite sure that we really believe it, and be willing to apply it to our own lives.—James Morrison (my dad)

One way to get to know the Lord and increase our faith in Him is by studying Scripture. It's an antidote to the teachings of the so-called "experts" who are trying to undermine our faith.

One tactic of such people is to engage in what they call "higher criticism." Perhaps a more accurate term for it would be, "trying to find intellectual excuses for not believing the Bible." Their theories forget something very important that should be obvious—the Bible tells us about real people in real life.

For example, these "scholars" analyze the vocabulary in Paul's epistles, and say that some of them must have a different author because the writing style and vocabulary are different. Well, in real life, people write differently based on who they are writing to and what they are writing about.

If those scholars analyzed the chapters I wrote in this book, they would conclude there were two authors, one who writes about Scripture, and another who writes about current events, using a different style and vocabulary. And they would attribute my poems to a third author. However, I can assure you I am only one person.

Think about your own life. Would you write to your boss the same way you would write to your spouse or your children? Would you write a love letter the same way that you write business correspondence? Of course not. These so-called "experts" have lost their common sense.

Such "scholars" also analyze the parables of Jesus, as presented in the Gospels and make a big deal out of the fact there are variations in the stories. They have forgotten something. Jesus was a real man, living a real life. The Bible shows Him constantly on the move, teaching in many places. In real life, traveling preachers tell the same stories many times, with variations in how they tell them.

Some "experts" also make a big deal out of the fact that two Gospels tell about blind Bartimaeus by himself, and one Gospel mentions two blind men, instead of just talking about Bartimaeus. If you were a blind beggar, wouldn't you hang out with other blind beggars? You would have a lot in common. They would understand you in a way that the rest of the world doesn't. So Bartimaeus was with a blind friend, and two Gospels just mention him, but the other Gospel mentions his friend as well. That is not a problem.

In real life, if several people witness the same event and write accounts about it, there is variation in the stories, because different people focus on different aspects of what happened. For example, were you ever with family members or friends when something notable happened, and then afterwards you heard different people talk about the event? Don't they emphasize different things? One person may major on something that another person doesn't even mention. That is what happens in everyday life.

If so-called "experts" give you sophisticated-sounding reasons for not believing what the Bible says, please don't let them undermine your faith. I'm speaking from personal experience. When I first came to know the Lord, I loved the Bible so much I went to a college that claimed to be Christian, and I majored in religion. My professors filled my head with that kind of nonsense. It destroyed my trust in Scripture and almost shipwrecked my faith in God. It took me many years to recover from that.

Here is something that helped restore my trust in Scripture. Sir William Ramsay is an archaeologist who spent years researching the historical statements made by the apostle Luke in the book of Acts. He even sailed the route that Paul sailed in order to test the accuracy of Luke's nautical statements. Ramsay wrote:

> Further study . . . showed that the book [Acts] could bear the most minute scrutiny as an authority for the facts of the Aegean world.[1]

> You may press the words of Luke in a degree beyond any other historian's and they stand the keenest scrutiny and the hardest treatment.[2]

> Acts may justly be quoted as a trustworthy historical authority.[3]

> Luke is a historian of the first rank.[4]

Getting to know God is a lifetime adventure, and the Bible is amazing. Many times I will read a familiar passage, and all at once it seems to jump off the page at me. Suddenly, I understand it in a way I had never understood it before. That is the Holy Spirit working in us.

Jesus promised He would always be with us. That includes helping us get to know Him better and love Him more:

> Go ye therefore, and teach all nations, baptizing them in the name of the Father, and of the Son, and of the Holy Ghost: Teaching them to observe all things whatsoever I have commanded you: and, *lo, I am with you always, even unto the end of the world.* (Matthew 28:19-20, emphasis added)

> Let your conversation be without covetousness; and be content with such things as ye have: for he hath said, *I will never leave thee, nor forsake thee.* (Hebrews 13:5, emphasis added)

Overshadowed
(A Hymn by Harry A. Ironside)

How desolate my life would be,
How dark and drear my nights and days,
If Jesus' face I did not see
To brighten all earth's weary ways.

Chorus: I'm overshadowed by His mighty love,
Love eternal, changeless pure,
Overshadowed by His mighty love,
Rest is mine, serene, secure

He died to ransom me from sin,
He lives to keep me day by day,
I'm overshadowed by His mighty love,
Love that brightens all my way.

With burdened heart I wandered long,
By grief and unbelief distressed;

But now I sing faith's happy song,
In Christ my Savior I am blest.

Now judgment fears no more alarm,
I dread not death, nor Satan's pow'r;
The world for me has lost its charm,
God's grace sustains me every hour.

I'm overshadowed by His mighty love,
Love eternal, changeless pure,
Overshadowed by His mighty love,
Rest is mine, serene, secure.[5]

12

LEARNING TO
TRUST GOD MORE

**O taste and see that the Lord is good: blessed
is the man that trusteth in him. (Psalm 34:8)**

In order to learn to trust someone, you have to get to know that person better. That includes spending time with him, and communicating with him. When it comes to God, we communicate through prayer and worship, and we learn about Him by reading the Bible, where He tells us a lot about Himself, and we see him act in the lives of His people.

I also find it helpful to read books about the lives of great men and women of faith. One of my favorites is Gladys Aylward, a missionary to China who had amazing adventures there, including taking a hundred children over the mountains to safety during the Japanese invasion of China during World War II. She was even able to reach the local Mandarin, who gave up his many wives and became a Christian. (A good biography is *The Small Woman*.) Another is Eric Liddell, the Olympic runner who became a missionary to China. (A good biography is *Complete Surrender*.)

Corrie ten Boom is a woman I greatly admire. *The Hiding Place* tells of her family's work with the Dutch underground during the Nazi occupation of Holland. She and her family smuggled Jews to safe places and hid Jews in their home. Eventually they were betrayed and sent to a German concentration camp. I recommend reading the book and getting the DVD. The book has a lot more information than you can put into a movie, but the movie enables you to see things in action. Corrie was there as a consultant when they made the movie, so it is very accurate. Knowing Corrie, she was praying all the time while the movie was being produced.

In My Father's House tells of Corrie and her family's lives before the war, how as a family, they had strong faith, regular prayer and Bible study, and the many ways they reached out to others. Among other things, Corrie led a Bible study for mentally handicapped children. After the war, Corrie wrote many books, and I have probably read them all. She talked so much about God's love and the ways He comes through for His people, giving many beautiful examples from her own life and from the lives of people she touched. There are three quotes from Corrie I often think about. They are:

Never be afraid to trust an unknown future to a known God.

There is no pit so deep He is not deeper still.

Worry does not deprive tomorrow of its sorrow. It deprives today of its strength.

All of us have blind spots and areas where our understanding is flawed or inadequate. The most important thing is whether or not we have a heart for God.

When we see Jesus face to face, the mistakes in our thinking will immediately disappear. The big question is, will we hear Him say, "Well done, thou good and faithful servant"? That depends on our hearts.

Here is an example from everyday life. Suppose a family has small children and a flower garden, and a young child picks some of those flowers to give to his mother because he loves her and wants to please her. Would a loving mother be delighted by this show of love? Or would she scold him for messing up the flower garden?

Sometimes we do things for God in ways that are comparable. We want to show love and do something for Him, but we don't have enough understanding to be able to take all of the factors into account.

When I was a little girl, I used to ask my mom if I could "holp" her cook dinner. Of course she said "yes," even though it meant there would be spills and messes, and it would take more time and trouble to make dinner than if she did it by herself. Sometimes when we are serving God we are like I was as a little girl, "holping" in the kitchen. We make messes because we don't know how to do things. That is part of the learning process.

Mom was happy when I "holped" her, and God likes it when we "holp" Him, too. And for the same reason. Love. While we are "holping," we are building relationship and learning.

Compared to God, we are just toddlers. If we can see ourselves and others as being like young children who are learning, then we can have more patience and show more grace when we (or they) make mistakes. This perspective also makes it easier to forgive.

Our understanding is valuable, but (as with little children) it is inadequate. The Bible says:

> Be not wise in thine own eyes: fear the Lord, and depart from evil. (Proverbs 3:7)

Our primary trust needs to be in God Himself, as opposed to our understanding of Him and of the world. The apostle Paul made this quite clear. He said:

> For the which cause I also suffer these things: nevertheless I am not ashamed: for I know *whom* I have believed, and

am persuaded that he is able to keep that which I have committed unto him against that day. (2 Timothy 1:12, emphasis added)

Notice that Paul said "whom," which means a person, namely God. He did not say "what," which would be a system of theology, interpretation of Scripture, his understanding of the world, and things like that. Paul's trust was in Almighty God—not in his own ability to figure things out.

Paul had an amazing experience, a revelation of Heaven. He saw and heard things he was not allowed to tell us about:

> I knew a man in Christ above fourteen years ago, (whether in the body, I cannot tell; or whether out of the body, I cannot tell: God knoweth;) such an one caught up to the third heaven. And I knew such a man, (whether in the body, or out of the body, I cannot tell: God knoweth;) How that he was caught up into paradise, and heard unspeakable words, which it is not lawful for a man to utter. (2 Corinthians 12:2-4)

However, Paul's trust was not in this experience or in those revelations. It was in Almighty God. He trusted a person (God) rather than his own experiences in Heaven. He openly told us he only knew "in part," that his understanding was limited:

> For *we know in part*, and we prophesy in part. (1 Corinthians 13:9, emphasis added)

> For now we see through a glass, darkly; but then face to face: now *I know in part;* but then shall I know even as also I am known. (1 Corinthians 13:12, emphasis added)

Paul was like a little boy who knows everything is going to be alright because his father is with him, and his father knows how to take care of things. And that's the way we need to be. That may be one of the things Jesus meant when He used the term "poor in spirit." He told us we should come to God like little children:

> Blessed are the poor in spirit: for theirs is the kingdom of heaven. (Matthew 5:3)

> Verily I say unto you, Except ye be converted, and become as little children, ye shall not enter into the kingdom of heaven. (Matthew 18:3)

That kind of humility and conscious dependence on God goes against the grain. Being fallen creatures sinful by nature, we want to think we have it all together and we know what we are doing. Well, that is partly true, but only partly. At our best, we are clumsy, and at times all of us become what the Bible calls "stiff necked" (stubborn and rebellious). That goes along with our sinful nature.

Even the best Christian is still just a sinner saved by grace. None of us will be fully right until we see Jesus face to face. And what a wonderful day that will be! The apostle John said:

> Beloved, now are we the sons of God, and it doth not yet appear what we shall be: but we know that, when he shall appear, we shall be like him; for we shall see him as he is. (1 John 3:2)

Paul said something that sounds very strange. I've wondered about it for years. I think I understand some aspects of it, but there is probably a lot more gold in this mine I haven't found yet. He stated:

> That I may know him, and the power of his resurrection, and the *fellowship of his sufferings*, being made conformable unto his death. (Philippians 3:10, emphasis added)

111

I can see why Paul wanted to know the power of Jesus' resurrection. But why would Paul want to know (or experience) the sufferings that Jesus went through? Or to somehow share in them?

Soldiers on the front lines go through traumatic things together. They share in the same sufferings, and sometimes they save one another's lives. There is a kind of bond soldiers can build with their battle buddies that cannot be developed under other circumstances. There is a closeness, a loyalty, and a willingness to lay down their lives for one another.

I remember reading about a battle during World War II when our troops were trapped, hemmed in by barbed wire, which made them sitting ducks—trapped and waiting to be killed by the Germans. Immediately, some of the soldiers ran full speed into that barbed wire, impaling themselves on it. That enabled the other soldiers to climb up over the barbed wire on the backs of their battle buddies. I cannot imagine the level of courage and dedication and loyalty and love that would be required to do something like that.

When we endure some of the things Jesus went through, to some extent that makes us become His battle buddy. It builds a relationship between us that cannot be built any other way. In Pastor Georgi Vins' life, this is what happened as he describes in his book *The Gospel in Bonds.* Pastor Vins was sent to Soviet gulags in the 1960s and 1970s for preaching the Gospel in communist USSR. While his suffering in prison was severe, this level of suffering drew him much closer to the Lord. They shared a "fellowship" of suffering.

GEORGI P. VINS

Suffering also gives us some idea of how much *He* was willing to suffer for us. What we go through is small compared to what Jesus suffered, but it is similar. A man with a broken foot has more understanding of what soldiers with amputated legs go through than a healthy runner does.

As we learn more about what Jesus was willing to go through in order to save us, we have more reasons to be grateful to Him, and it increases our trust in Him. If He loved us enough to suffer like that for us, then we can trust Him to do what is best for us.

Another thing that increases our trust is when we see God protect us. For example, one time I was at a stop light in front of a curved suspension bridge. Its curve was so high I couldn't see what was on the other side of the bridge. I was in the left turn lane, waiting for the arrow to make my turn. When I got the green arrow, I started to turn. But then somehow I felt I should not move, that I needed to stay there. So I did. And a few seconds later, a big truck came barreling down the bridge. He must have run the red light on the other side of the bridge. If I had made my turn when the green arrow came on, I would have been right in his path. I would have been crushed by that big truck.

That is one time when God saved my life and I am aware of it. How many other times has God rescued me when I wasn't aware of it? I won't find out until I get to Heaven.

Another thing that builds trust is when we are cornered, we have our back to the wall, and if God doesn't come through for us, then we've had it. Then God does come through. He rescues us, and that teaches us to trust Him more.

For example, I used to work in a neighborhood that was dangerous at night. Because I didn't have a car, I had to take a bus to get home. One day, my job required me to work so late that it was very dark when I left the office. The street was deserted, except for one man. As soon as he noticed me, he headed in my direction. That did not look good. Since he was between me and the office building, I couldn't run back to the office for refuge.

That man came closer and closer, and I became more and more frightened. Just then, a man walked out of my office building and came straight towards us, walking quickly. I think he probably noticed my perilous situation. As soon as he got near us, the other man ran away. The man from the office stayed with me until my bus arrived.

That was close timing, and I believe God was behind it. He can "nudge" people to do things. He has ways of getting people where they need to be (like a sheep dog does with sheep). My mom used to call that kind of thing "God's choreography." (God knows how to get people in the right place at the right time, and do it in complex ways when needed.)

You may ask, "What if that man had not rescued me? What if I had been raped?" Remember Romans 8:28. It includes *everything*—no exceptions:

> And we know that *all* things work together for good to them that love God, to them who are the called according to his purpose. (Romans 8:28, emphasis added)

In the case of rape, another Scripture applies. God brought this to my mind when I was praying with a friend who had been raped by a homosexual man when he was five years old. In context, Jesus was talking about food. However, the principle applies to other things as well, including rape:

> There is nothing from without a man, that entering into him can defile him. (Mark 7:15)

No matter what we go through, God is willing and able to heal our hearts and comfort us:

> He healeth the broken in heart, and bindeth up their wounds. (Psalm 147:3)

> For the Lamb which is in the midst of the throne shall feed them, and shall lead them unto living fountains of waters: and God shall wipe away all tears from their eyes. (Revelation 7:17)

In addition, there is an important principle that the apostle Paul told us about:

> Who comforteth us in all our tribulation, that we may be able to comfort them which are in any trouble, by the comfort wherewith we ourselves are comforted of God. (2 Corinthians 1:4)

When we go through bad things, God is able to heal us and comfort us. And then we are able to help and comfort others who go through similar things.

For example, I'm a widow. Because of that, I understand other widows in a way that women whose husbands are still alive can't. It also gives me understanding of anybody who has had a death in the family, and I can comfort them in ways that other people can't do.

As I referred to a little earlier in this chapter, in communist Russia, Christians were severely persecuted. They endured tremendous suffering, both physical and psychological. Those who were faithful to God became sweeter, more gentle, and more devoted. They came closer to God, instead of becoming bitter and turning away from Him. (The biography *A Small Price to Pay* by Harvey Yoder tells about one family who went through that.) I've heard similar stories about persecuted Christians in China.

Remember Shadrach, Meshach, and Abednego? They knew God was able to deliver them, but their faithfulness did not depend on being rescued:

> If it be so, our God whom we serve is able to deliver us from the burning fiery furnace, and he will deliver us out of thine hand, O king. But if not, be it known unto thee, O king, that we will not serve thy gods, nor worship the golden image which thou hast set up. (Daniel 3:17-18)

They knew God had the power to save them, but they were determined to be faithful, even if it meant being burned alive. Their loyalty to God and their trust in Him did not depend on whether or not He rescued them from that situation. And that's the way we need to be.

Hebrews 11 tells about men and women who had great faith. People like to read about miracles God did for heroes of the faith such as Abraham and Moses. However, the last five verses tell of heroes who were tortured and martyred for their faith. The transition occurs in verse 35:

> Women received their dead raised to life again: and others were tortured, not accepting deliverance; that they might obtain a better resurrection. (Hebrews 11:35)

When God miraculously heals somebody or raises them from the dead, we admire His power and are grateful for His love. However, I suspect it takes even more power for Him to enable a frail human being to endure being tortured to death, trusting in God while he goes through it, and praying for his persecutors instead of hating them. For example, Stephen prayed for the people who were stoning him to death while they were doing it:

> Then they cried out with a loud voice, and stopped their ears, and ran upon him with one accord, And cast him out of the city, and stoned him: and the witnesses laid down their clothes at a young man's feet, whose name was Saul. And they stoned Stephen, calling upon God, and saying, Lord Jesus, receive my spirit. And he kneeled down, and cried with a loud voice, Lord, lay not this sin to their charge. And when he had said this, he fell asleep. (Acts 7:57-60)

Notice that Saul (Paul) was there when this happened. I wonder if that contributed to his conversion. Since he was there at the time, Paul is one of the men Stephen prayed for.

If we are able to avoid being harmed by others, without compromising our faith, then we should do so. Paul avoided a Roman whipping. He had been whipped by the Jews, but that was limited to 39 lashes. With the Romans, there was no limit, and some people died from those whippings. Here is how Paul avoided it by using Roman law:

> The chief captain commanded him to be brought into the castle, and bade that he should be examined by scourging; that he might know wherefore they cried so against him. And as they bound him with thongs, Paul said unto the centurion that stood by, Is it lawful for you to scourge a man that is a Roman, and uncondemned? When the centurion heard that, he went and told the chief captain, saying, Take heed what thou doest: for this man is a Roman. Then the chief captain came, and said unto him, Tell me, art thou a Roman? He said, Yea. And the chief captain answered, With a great sum obtained I this freedom. And Paul said, But I was free born. Then straightway they departed from him which should have examined him: and the chief captain also was afraid, after he knew that he was a Roman, and because he had bound him. (Acts 22:24-29)

So we should be prudent and avoid unnecessary suffering. At the same time, if we do suffer, then we can look to see how Jesus went through similar things, and share in the "fellowship of his sufferings."

It's a win/win situation. It's good to avoid suffering and hardship if we can do so without denying God. However, if we go through it, then that will bring us closer to God, if we respond biblically. And that will increase our trust and faith in God, and our love for Him.

That brings me back to Romans 8:28, which is a verse that has had a profound influence on my life. We are never at the mercy of men or of circumstances because God is willing and able to make everything work out for our long-term, eternal good, if we love Him. No exceptions.

God gives us grace and blessing in His real world, in the present moment. If we get lost in the past (through regrets, or wishing we were back in "the good old days," or in other ways), we won't find God's blessing there. If we get lost in the future (through fears, or hopes, or wishful thinking), we won't find His grace there, either. And we won't find it when we are daydreaming or lost in some imaginary world.

When Corrie ten Boom was a little girl, she asked her father what it was like to die. He replied by asking Corrie, "When we go to the train station, when do I give you your ticket?"

She replied, "When I am getting on the train." Corrie's father used that example to teach her that God gives us His grace at the very moment we need it—not ahead of time.

That's a good thing, because otherwise our trust would be in having "grace in the bank" instead of trusting in God Himself. Good parents want to develop and strengthen their relationship with their children, and our Father in Heaven does the same with His children.

God knows the right timing for things. He is always with us. He will never leave us, or forget us, or fail to take care of us. However, He often does it at the very last minute.

God will get us through whatever we have to go through. When it is all over, then He will comfort us and heal us. Some day we will be in Heaven, with Resurrection bodies, and God will wipe away all our tears:

> Can a woman forget her sucking child, that she should not have compassion on the son of her womb? yea, they may forget, yet will I not forget thee. (Isaiah 49:15)

> And the ransomed of the Lord shall return, and come to Zion with songs and everlasting joy upon their heads: they shall obtain joy and gladness, and sorrow and sighing shall flee away. (Isaiah 35:10)

"Trust"
By Georgi Vins

Very often upon my life's journey
Obstacles like mountains would arise
Sealing off the expanses of heaven
And my pathway that leads to the skies.

Storms shrieked of death and destruction
And there seemed no appeasing their lust;
Then I heard, from those pages so sacred,
Whispers, "Trust" and again, "Only trust!"

In the midst of the tempest's fierce howling
When the tumult was too much to bear,
From His Word I would hear God's voice speaking,
"You'll find power though prayer—
yes, through prayer!"

So I trusted and walked on unswerving,
And to quiet the storm I would pray;
Then the mountains obstructing my pathway
Meekly trembled and faded away.

Pastor Georgi Vins was imprisoned for eight years
in Soviet prison camps for his faith. His book, *The
Gospel in Bonds*, is his account of his prison years.
This poem is from that book; used with permission.

[B]e renewed in the spirit of your mind; and that ye put on the new man, which after God is created in righteousness and true holiness. (Ephesians 4:20-24)

13

DON'T GIVE THE DEVIL A BEACHHEAD

Neither give place to the devil. (Ephesians 4:27)

Not giving "place" to the devil means that we shouldn't give the devil a beachhead from which he can launch an attack against us. That would also enable the devil to use us to try to harm other people, or to influence them in bad ways. We see an example of that when Jesus told Peter, "Get thee behind me, Satan" (Matthew 16:23).

The Bible talks about the dangers of long-term anger. Now there is such a thing as righteous anger. We see it when Jesus drove the money changers out of the temple (John 2:13-17).

Jesus became angry about a bad situation, and He did something to make it right. However, He was not an angry man. He was a man who was known primarily for His love and compassion. The Bible warns us not to associate with angry men (or women):

> Make no friendship with an angry man; and with a furious man thou shalt not go. (Proverbs 22:24)

The point is this. Is anger an identifying mark of our character? Or is it something that shows up occasionally, and appropriately, and then departs quickly? God gave us the emotion of anger for a reason. There are times when it is needed.

Here is an example from my life. Many years ago, I was a live-in housemother in a home for mentally challenged adults. A young man came to visit. (He had been in the same institution the people in our group home came from.) Within ten minutes, he had all of our people so upset they were verbally attacking one another. He was a catalyst for discord, confusion, and strife. He finally left, and after a while, our people calmed down again.

I made some inquiries and learned this young man had a reputation for being a troublemaker. And he was dangerous. He had put some counselors in the hospital.

A few weeks later, he showed up again. When I saw him coming up the sidewalk, I turned into a momma bear who was defending her cubs. I was so angry I didn't care if he put me in the hospital. That boy was NOT going to get into our home again. I confronted him, and he left without hurting me. And he never came back.

I was so angry at that young man I was willing to risk being injured by him, even to the point of having to be hospitalized. However, I didn't remain angry. Once he was gone, I forgot about him and went back to being a loving housemother.

When anger remains with us, it becomes spiritually dangerous. It can lead us to do sinful things. It can also give the devil a beachhead from which he can attack us (tempt us, confuse us, influence us, etc.):

> Be ye angry, and sin not: let not the sun go down upon your wrath: Neither give place to the devil. (Ephesians 4:26-27)

If we remain angry, then we are in danger of becoming bitter, and according to the Bible, bitterness defiles us. In addition, it is contagious. Our bitterness can cause others to become defiled:

> Looking diligently lest any man fail of the grace of God;
> lest any root of bitterness springing up trouble you, and
> thereby many be defiled. (Hebrews 12:15)

Anger is a strong emotion that can take over and cause us to do harmful things. This is the opposite of being "sober" and "vigilant." Think about people who are drunk. They get carried away by their emotions, and it is easy for them to lose the ability to be alert. Sometimes this can cause practical problems (for example, when they are driving). We cannot afford to be in that state of mind because we have an enemy who is looking for opportunities to harm us:

> Be sober, be vigilant; because your adversary the devil,
> as a roaring lion, walketh about, seeking whom he may
> devour. (1 Peter 5:8)

The Bible tells us God is "slow to anger," and He wants us to be the same way. Getting angry quickly and easily causes problems. In contrast, being "slow to anger" is a virtue:

> The Lord is gracious, and full of compassion; slow to
> anger, and of great mercy. (Psalm 145:8)

> He that is slow to anger is better than the mighty; and he
> that ruleth his spirit than he that taketh a city. (Proverbs
> 16:32)

> He that is soon angry dealeth foolishly. (Proverbs 14:17)

"Wrath" is stronger than ordinary anger. The Bible warns us to avoid wrath because it can make us do ungodly things:

> A wrathful man stirreth up strife: but he that is slow to
> anger appeaseth strife. (Proverbs 15:18)

> Wherefore, my beloved brethren, let every man be swift to hear, slow to speak, *slow to wrath:* For the wrath of man worketh not the righteousness of God. (James 1:19-20, emphasis added)

Wrath can have serious consequences. The apostle Paul calls it a work of the flesh and says it can lead to damnation (remember Galatians 5:19-21 from page 85). In that portion of Scripture, Paul lists "wrath" right along with sins like adultery, witchcraft, idolatry, and murder. That makes it very serious. He then contrasts such things with the "fruit of the Spirit":

> But the fruit of the Spirit is love, joy, peace, long-suffering, gentleness, goodness, faith, Meekness, temperance: against such there is no law. And they that are Christ's have crucified the flesh with the affections and lusts. (Galatians 5:22-24)

There is a competition between the "flesh" (our carnal nature) and the Spirit. An ongoing struggle between them exists. Our carnal nature makes it difficult for us to live the way that God wants us to live. We want to do the right thing, but our "flesh" gets in the way:

> This I say then, Walk in the Spirit, and ye shall not fulfil the lust of the flesh. For the flesh lusteth against the Spirit, and the Spirit against the flesh: and these are contrary the one to the other: so that ye cannot do the things that ye would. (Galatians 5:16-17)

There is an old story about a man who told his friend, "I feel like there are two dogs fighting inside of me."

His friend asked, "Which one is winning?"

And he replied, "The one I feed the most."

We need to feed the godly side of us and starve the carnal side. Prayer, worship, Scripture, and the fellowship of solid Christian friends help feed the godly side.

There is an expression, "nursing a grudge." According to *Webster's Dictionary*, a grudge is "a feeling of deep-seated resentment or ill will." In other words, it's a form of long-term anger.

Think about what a nursing mother does. She looks at her baby, feeds him, caresses him, and talks to him. She becomes totally focused on that baby and nourishes him so he can grow big and strong.

What does it mean to "nurse a grudge"? To keep feeding it, and thinking about it, and focusing on it. Of course, that makes it keep growing. It gets bigger and stronger.

That is the exact opposite of what we should do as Christians. We should starve that grudge and do everything we can to kill it. We cannot afford to have long-term anger. That gives the devil a beachhead, which is spiritually dangerous for us. In addition, when the devil is able to work on us, then we may wind up hurting other people.

Long-term anger can take the form of resentment. Sometimes it can appear to be "righteous indignation." The problem is, if it remains—if it continues—then it stops being righteous.

Long-term anger can also take the form of being offended. If somebody does something offensive, that does not mean we have to become offended. As Christians, we need to learn to respond biblically instead of reacting carnally. It's a learning process that requires time, thought, and prayer. It's a skill that is developed in us as we learn to walk in the Spirit and as we learn to surrender our sins and weaknesses to the Lord.

Think about the term "to take offense." Somebody does something hurtful, something to offend you. Well, picture that as being like an object the person just put on the table in front of you. He or she put it there. But it is up to you to decide whether or not to "take" it. Are you going to pick it up? Or are you going to leave it there?

We do not have to take offense just because somebody does something offensive to us. We can choose not to take offense. We can choose to leave it alone.

Anger can also take the form of being annoyed, exasperated, frustrated, or indignant. We all have times of feeling that way. As long as it is only temporary, and we don't do anything sinful as a result of it, that's all right. However, if it continues—if it becomes long-term—then we have a problem.

When we are angry, it is easy for us to say and do things that hurt other people. If the ones we hurt are Christians, then God counts it as having done those things to Jesus Christ.

We see this when Jesus appeared to Saul when he was on the road to Damascus. (Paul was called Saul before he became a Christian.) Paul had been actively persecuting Christians, but Jesus said that Paul had been persecuting Him (Jesus).

> And he fell to the earth, and heard a voice saying unto him, Saul, Saul, why persecutest thou *me?* And he said, Who art thou, Lord? And the Lord said, *I am Jesus whom thou persecutest:* it is hard for thee to kick against the pricks. (Acts 9:4-5, emphasis added)

One form that long-term anger can take is self-condemnation. For some people, this is a real problem. We sinned. We repented. God forgave us. He took our sins away from us. The Bible says:

> He hath not dealt with us after our sins; nor rewarded us according to our iniquities. For as the heaven is high above the earth, so great is his mercy toward them that fear him. *As far as the east is from the west, so far hath he removed our transgressions from us.* Like as a father pitieth his children, so the Lord pitieth them that fear him. (Psalm 103:10-13, emphasis added)

East and west never meet. No matter how far you travel east, you never wind up going west. That is very different from north and south, which meet at the North Pole and the South Pole.

God goes even further than that. Once we repent and He forgives us, then He doesn't even remember our sins. He told us:

> I, even I, am he that blotteth out thy transgressions for mine own sake, and will not remember thy sins. (Isaiah 43:25)

> He will turn again, he will have compassion upon us; he will subdue our iniquities; and thou wilt cast all their sins into the depths of the sea. (Micah 7:19)

Now if God has put away our sins, and He doesn't remember them anymore, then who are we to keep dredging them up and beating ourselves up about them? This can actually be a form of pride. It is saying our standards are higher than God's standards are.

Remember Jesus said, "Inasmuch as ye have done it unto one of the least of these my brethren, ye have done it unto me." (Matthew 25:40) Because we are Christians, that applies to us as much as to other people. When we keep beating ourselves over the heads for sins that God has already forgiven, then we are tormenting one of God's people (namely ourselves). God counts that as doing it to Jesus.

The apostle Paul must have struggled with that problem. Before he became a Christian, he rounded up Christians and had them put to death. He must have encountered many Christians who knew people or were related to people who Paul was responsible for killing. But Paul concluded:

> Brethren, I count not myself to have apprehended: but this one thing I do, *forgetting those things which are behind,* and reaching forth unto those things which are before,

I press toward the mark for the prize of the high calling of God in Christ Jesus. (Philippians 3:13-14, emphasis added)

One of the things Paul had to put behind him and not look back at was his past sin of persecuting Christians.

We need to forgive everybody. That includes ourselves.

In the book of Revelation, the devil is called "the accuser of the brethren" (Revelation 12:10). Why should we do the devil's job for him?

We need to forgive others instead of accusing them. And once we have repented of our sins then we need to stop accusing ourselves.

The conviction of the Holy Spirit draws us closer to God. It gets us to focus on Him and repent of our sins. In contrast, self-condemnation gets us to focus on ourselves instead of God.

When it comes to our sins, there are two traps we can fall into. One trap is to ignore our sins or deny them or not take them seriously. The other trap is to keep hitting ourselves over the heads because of them, long after we have repented of them and God has forgotten them. We need to avoid both traps.

Some people have such a serious problem with self-condemnation that acknowledging their sins has become unbearable for them. And as a result, they deny their sins.

The answer to that problem is to treat self-condemnation as being some of the "fiery darts" the enemy throws at us (Ephesians 6:16). We need to consciously refuse to play that game. We need to get our focus off of ourselves and back on to God. We need to develop the discipline of refusing to get into self-condemnation.

This becomes especially important during times of persecution, because the world will keep accusing us. And not just for our faults. It will condemn the good things we say and do. It will call good things evil. God said:

> Woe unto them that call evil good, and good evil; that put
> darkness for light, and light for darkness; that put bitter
> for sweet, and sweet for bitter! (Isaiah 5:20)

God would not have said that if people didn't do it. And unfortunately, they do. It has become widespread in America. It is being done by the media, by the entertainment industry, and by teachers in public schools and universities.

It is also being done by some psychiatrists. For example, Dr. Brock Chisholm wants to destroy our ability to tell the difference between good and evil. He is the psychiatrist who was the first Secretary-General of the United Nations' World Health Organization, so he is in a position of great power and influence. He is one of the people that Psalm 2 talks about:

> The kings of the earth set themselves, and the rulers take
> counsel together, against the LORD, and against his
> anointed. (Psalm 2:2)

Dr. Chisholm and the other ungodly "movers and shakers" who have an anti-Christian agenda have no idea of what is at stake for them. It does not pay to mess with God. Unless they wake up and repent, they will come to a bad end.

When I was a girl, the only evil people I knew about were the ones I read about in books. I also saw bad guys in cowboy movies on TV. Those were people from other countries or other times. They were not in my real world. Unfortunately, things have changed. Today, I often read about evil people in the news, and sometimes I run into them in person.

If persecution increases, then we may see terrible things done by wicked people. If that happens, we will have to be on guard against long-term anger. Of course, anger will rise up in us from time to time, but we cannot afford to let it remain because it is sin.

There is an old saying that "You can't keep a bird from flying overhead, but you can keep it from building a nest in your hair."

The same is true of anger. We can't help getting angry at times, but we don't have to stay angry.

One good antidote to anger is to remember that God is going to take care of the bad guys. They will pay for what they are doing—unless they repent and get saved, which would be much better. Jesus died to save them. He paid a terrible price in order to enable them to be saved, and He should get what He paid for. So we should pray for their salvation.

It is always wonderful to hear testimonies of terrorists, hit men, drug dealers, and nasty bikers who become Christians. I love it when really bad guys get saved. That demonstrates what a mighty God we serve. Once they become Christians, such people are as zealous and bold for God as they used to be for doing bad things.

However, if they do not get saved, then God will deal with them. So for us, it's a win/win situation. If they get saved, then we will have a new brother or sister in Christ, and we can be reconciled. And if they don't, God will punish them for the evil they have done to us and to others. They will pay a heavy price for it.

In the following Scripture quotation, the term "give place unto wrath" means leaving room for God's wrath, as opposed to ours. God can have wrath that is absolutely righteous, because He is holy. But we are sinful people, even though we have been saved by grace. Therefore, when we get angry (especially if it gets to the point of "wrath"), it is easy for us to fall into sin. So it is better (and spiritually much safer) to leave the wrath to God:

> Dearly beloved, avenge not yourselves, but rather give place unto wrath: for it is written, Vengeance is mine; I will repay, saith the Lord. (Romans 12:19)

There are many places in the Bible that talk about how God deals with wicked men and those who do evil things. Here are a few of them:

The ungodly are not so: but are like the chaff which the wind driveth away. Therefore the ungodly shall not stand in the judgment, nor sinners in the congregation of the righteous. For the Lord knoweth the way of the righteous: but the way of the ungodly shall perish. (Psalm 1:4-6)

Thou hast rebuked the heathen, thou hast destroyed the wicked, thou hast put out their name for ever and ever. (Psalm 9:5)

Surely thou didst set them in slippery places: thou castedst them down into destruction. How are they brought into desolation, as in a moment! they are utterly consumed with terrors." (Psalm 73:18-19)

I have seen the wicked in great power, and spreading himself like a green bay tree. Yet he passed away, and, lo, he was not: yea, I sought him, but he could not be found. (Psalm 37:35-36)

Rest in the Lord, and wait patiently for him: fret not thyself because of him who prospereth in his way, because of the man who bringeth wicked devices to pass. Cease from anger, and forsake wrath: fret not thyself in any wise to do evil. For evildoers shall be cut off: but those that wait upon the Lord, they shall inherit the earth. For yet a little while, and the wicked shall not be: yea, thou shalt diligently consider his place, and it shall not be. But the meek shall inherit the earth; and shall delight themselves in the abundance of peace. (Psalm 37:7-11)

According to *Webster's Dictionary*, the word "meek" means "enduring injury with patience and without resentment." It can also mean "submissive," but the primary meaning is what the Bible calls being "longsuffering." I have seen it defined as being "strength under control."[1] To put it in terms of animals, "meek" does not mean being a helpless mouse. It means being a patient lion.

A good antidote to anger is to major on learning to love, as love is described in the Bible. (Sometimes the Bible refers to love as "charity.") Love should be the hallmark of a Christian:

> By this shall all men know that ye are my disciples, if ye have love one to another. (John 13:35)

> Charity suffereth long, and is kind; charity envieth not; charity vaunteth not itself, is not puffed up, Doth not behave itself unseemly, seeketh not her own, *is not easily provoked,* thinketh no evil; Rejoiceth not in iniquity, but rejoiceth in the truth; Beareth all things, believeth all things, hopeth all things, endureth all things. (1 Corinthians 13:4-7, emphasis added)

> Put on therefore, as the elect of God, holy and beloved, bowels of *mercies,* kindness, humbleness of mind, meekness, *longsuffering;* Forbearing one another, and *forgiving one another,* if any man have a quarrel against any: even as *Christ forgave you, so also do ye.* And above all these things put on charity, which is the bond of perfectness. And let the peace of God rule in your hearts, to the which also ye are called in one body; and be ye thankful. (Colossians 3:12-15, emphasis added)

When it comes to serious persecution, there isn't much we can do about the bad guys. Jews who survived the Holocaust know that. So do the Middle Eastern Christians who live in nations where Christians are being beheaded and burned alive. In extreme situations like that, all we can do is endure the hardship and trust the Lord:

> Thou therefore endure hardness, as a good soldier of Jesus Christ." (2 Timothy 2:3)

> He shall not be afraid of evil tidings: his heart is fixed, trusting in the Lord. (Psalm 112:7)

Could something like that happen in America and Canada? It's possible. No nation is immune to such things if it turns away from God. Unfortunately, there are many parallels between modern North America and Germany in the days before Hitler became a full-fledged dictator.

Thankfully, we are never at the mercy of men or of circumstances because God is able to make *all* things work out for our long-term, eternal good if we love Him. And He promises us that nothing at all can separate us from His love.

We will go through some difficult things. At times, we won't understand why these things are happening or how it is possible for them to happen. That is when it is good to remind ourselves that only God sees the big picture.

Paul described our lives as Christians as being like people who are running in a race—and runners have to look forward. If they look back while they are running, then they will slow down, and they are in danger of running into someone or tripping over something. They have to keep looking forward:

Wherefore seeing we also are compassed about with so great a cloud of witnesses, let us lay aside every weight, and the sin which doth so easily beset us, and let us *run with patience the race that is set before us*, Looking unto Jesus the author and finisher of our faith; who for the joy that was set before him endured the cross, despising the shame, and is set down at the right hand of the throne of God. (Hebrews 12:1-2, emphasis added)

And whatsoever ye do in word or deed, do all in the name of the Lord Jesus, giving thanks to God and the Father by him. (Colossians 3: 17)

14

GIVING THANKS TO GOD

In every thing give thanks: for this is the will of God in Christ Jesus concerning you. (1 Thessalonians 5:18)

heard about an old woman with painful arthritis who struggled to climb a hill. When she got to the top, she looked at the view and said, "God, why did You make the world so beautiful?"

I'm afraid that many of us would have been complaining about the pain and the difficulty in walking, instead of giving thanks for the beauty. I've been guilty of doing that kind of thing myself.

When we are suffering, it is so easy to tell God, "It's not fair! Why did You let this happen to me?" But how often do we turn to God and say, "Why did You save me? I deserved to go to Hell. Why do You love me when I have been so unfaithful to you? Why are You so patient with me when I become stubborn and rebellious?"

It's so easy to take good things for granted and to focus on our problems. Our default setting seems to be self-pity and a sense of entitlement.

The Bible has a lot to say about the importance of praise and thanksgiving. Here are a few examples:

> Rejoice in the Lord always: and again I say, Rejoice . . . Be careful [anxious] for nothing; but in every thing by prayer and supplication with thanksgiving let your requests be made known unto God. And the peace of God, which passeth all understanding, shall keep your hearts and minds through Christ Jesus. (Philippians 4:4-7)

> Rejoice evermore. Pray without ceasing. In every thing give thanks: for this is the will of God in Christ Jesus concerning you. (1 Thessalonians 5:16-18)

> O Lord, open thou my lips; and my mouth shall shew forth thy praise. (Psalm 51:15)

God created us and gave us a beautiful world in which to live. After Adam and Eve fell into sin, Jesus died on the Cross to save us. And God has Heaven waiting for us. Compared to those blessings, anything we suffer now is small and temporary. The apostle Paul said:

> For our light affliction, which is but for a moment, worketh for us a far more exceeding and eternal weight of glory. (2 Corinthians 4:17)

Let us consider some of the things Paul calls a "light" affliction. At one point, Paul went through something so severe he "despaired even of life" (2 Corinthians 1:8). Here is what Paul says about his sufferings and persecutions:

> Of the Jews five times received I forty stripes save one. Thrice was I beaten with rods, once was I stoned, thrice I suffered shipwreck, a night and a day I have been in the deep; In journeyings often, in perils of waters, in perils of robbers, in perils by mine own countrymen, in perils by the heathen, in perils in the city, in perils in the wilderness, in perils in the sea, in perils among false brethren; In weariness and painfulness, in watchings

often, in hunger and thirst, in fastings often, in cold and nakedness. (2 Corinthians 11:24-27)

I would not want to have to go through any of these sufferings, but Christians in countries with severe persecution suffer many similar things.

We need to be prepared to endure such things ourselves, if necessary. We also need to have Paul's perspective about them. That is biblical, and it is based on reality—on the nature and character of God and the importance of eternity.

Lack of gratitude to God can result in serious consequences. In the first chapter of Paul's epistle to the Romans, we see a horrible downhill spiral. It's a slippery slope, which escalates into depravity and destruction. The starting point is a lack of gratitude and respect for God. In the beginning, they knew God, but they refused to give Him glory, and they were not thankful.

> lack of gratitude to God can result in serious consequences—it's a slippery slope, which escalates into depravity and destruction

It gets to the point where they "did not like to retain God in their knowledge." In other words, they used to know that God is real. Deep down inside, they still know it. In spite of that, they deny God's existence. They try to find reasons for not believing in Him.

That would explain why we see militant atheists who hate God. How can you hate somebody who doesn't exist? At some level, they know better. Otherwise, they would not be able to hate Him. There are even some atheists who say they want to "kill the God of Christianity."[1]

Here is the apostle Paul's description of this deadly downhill slide:

Because that, when they knew God, they glorified him not as God, neither were thankful; but became vain in their imaginations, and their foolish heart was darkened.

Professing themselves to be wise, they became fools, And changed the glory of the uncorruptible God into an image made like to corruptible man, and to birds, and fourfooted beasts, and creeping things. Wherefore God also gave them up to uncleanness through the lusts of their own hearts, to dishonour their own bodies between themselves: Who changed the truth of God into a lie, and worshipped and served the creature more than the Creator, who is blessed for ever. Amen. (Romans 1:21-25)

With such godlessness and self-worship, people sink into unimaginable depravity, as Paul explains:

For this cause God gave them up unto vile affections: for even their women did change the natural use into that which is against nature: And likewise also the men, leaving the natural use of the woman, burned in their lust one toward another; men with men working that which is unseemly, and receiving in themselves that recompence of their error which was meet. And even as *they did not like to retain God in their knowledge,* God gave them over to a reprobate mind . . . Being filled with all unrighteousness, fornication, wickedness, covetousness, maliciousness; full of envy, murder, debate, deceit, malignity; whisperers, Backbiters, haters of God, despiteful, proud, boasters, *inventors of evil things* . . . Who knowing the judgment of God, that they which commit such things are worthy of death, not only do the same, but have pleasure in them that do them. (Romans 1:26-32, emphasis added)

Unfortunately, this is a good description of where much of the Western world is today. We see many people in various stages of this downhill slide. The media and the entertainment industry actively promote it. So do our public schools.

The antidote is to have a grateful heart and to give thanks to God. This does not come naturally. We have to develop the habit of giving thanks.

Have you ever noticed that people who complain keep finding more and more things to complain about? In contrast, people who are thankful keep finding more and more reasons to give thanks.

We have a choice to make. Either we can become more and more grateful to God, or else we can become more and more full of complaining and self-pity. Eventually, that can end in becoming bitter. The Bible warns us that bitterness is both deadly and contagious: "lest any root of bitterness springing up trouble you, and thereby many be defiled" (Hebrews 12:15).

Praising God and giving thanks to Him increases our faith. It also makes us more aware of God's presence, His love, His power, and His faithfulness. Lack of praise and gratitude hinders our relationship with God. That makes us more vulnerable to doubts and temptations.

To put it in medical terms, you could say that praise and thanksgiving strengthen our spiritual immune system. It protects us both spiritually and emotionally. It helps us grow stronger and have more energy and focus to live biblically and do whatever God has called us to do.

Praising God and showing gratitude to Him can take many forms. One is singing hymns and worship songs. The Bible strongly encourages us to do that:

> Speaking to yourselves in psalms and hymns and spiritual songs, singing and making melody in your heart to the Lord; Giving thanks always for all things unto God and the Father in the name of our Lord Jesus Christ. (Ephesians 5:19 20)

This means more than singing in church. It means singing when we are driving, or washing the dishes, or taking a shower. And it means singing "in our hearts" (silently) in addition to singing out loud.

I have a friend who memorizes a lot of Scripture, and he praises the Lord by quoting Scripture or talking to God in biblical terms. He uses Scripture passages appropriate for the situation he is in at the moment.

I knew a mentally handicapped lady named Nancy whose mental age was about two years old. She loved God so much. If she saw a Bible, she would pick it up and stroke it and hold it against her heart.

She was unable to read, but she knew the Bible was God's Word, and she loved it. One day somebody gave her a painting of Jesus. She kissed it and started dancing. Nancy was not able to express herself verbally, so she showed her joy and love and gratitude by dancing.

Eric Liddell, the famous Olypmic runner, said that when he ran, he could feel God's pleasure. He ran in order to glorify God and to please God. After he won the Olympics, Eric became a missionary in China. His fame as an athlete gave him a platform for telling people about Jesus. They came to see the famous runner, but they wound up learning about God. Liddell knew the importance of having a thankful and praiseful heart. In 1945 during World War II, while on the mission field, he was sent to an internment camp. One fellow internee who survived the war, wrote a book and said: [Eric Liddell] "was the finest Christian gentleman it has been my pleasure to meet. In all the time in the camp, I never heard him say a bad word about anybody." During his internment, Liddell maintained a heart toward God, often helping and encouraging others. He died in February 1945 while still imprisoned.

There is another way to praise and glorify God. Because persecution is increasing, many of us will be called to do it.

Eric Liddell at Xiaochang, China during World War 2
where he was crossing Japanese lines to bring aid to
the Chinese. © Eric Liddell Centre.

This can take many forms. The most extreme is when Christians in the Middle East are told to renounce their faith or be killed. In North America, right now it is more likely to be the challenge to either acknowledge or else deny biblical truths and biblical morality. For example, as I stated before, a Christian baker in America refused to bake a wedding cake for a homosexual wedding. The judge told the baker that this violates the antidiscrimination law of Colorado, and unless he bakes cakes for homosexual weddings, he will be fined and he may even be sent to prison.

Another way to glorify God is to die for Him. Some people are called to be martyrs. Jesus made it clear it was God's will for Peter to be martyred:

> Verily, verily, I say unto thee, When thou wast young, thou girdest thyself, and walkedst whither thou wouldest: but when thou shalt be old, thou shalt stretch forth thy hands, and another shall gird thee, and carry thee whither thou wouldest not. This spake he, *signifying by what death he should glorify God.* And when he had spoken this, he saith unto him, Follow me. (John 21:18-19, emphasis added)

The Bible tells us to protect ourselves and our families from persecution if we can do so without denying Him: "But when they persecute you in this city, flee ye into another" (Matthew 10:23).

However, we need to be willing to die for Him if necessary. We need to love God more than we love our lives:

> Precious in the sight of the Lord is the death of his saints. (Psalm 116:15)

> And they overcame him by the blood of the Lamb, and by the word of their testimony; and they loved not their lives unto the death. (Revelation 12:11)

LIGHT AFTER DARKNESS
(by Frances Ridley Havergal, 1879)

Light after darkness, gain after loss,
Strength after suffering, crown after cross.
Sweet after bitter, song after sigh,
Home after wandering, praise after cry.

Sheaves after sowing, sun after rain,
Sight after mystery, peace after pain.
Joy after sorrow, calm after blast,
Rest after weariness, sweet rest at last.

Near after distant, gleam after gloom,
Love after loneliness, life after tomb.
After long agony, rapture of bliss!
Right was the pathway leading to this!

15

JESUS TOLD US TO FORGIVE

**And when ye stand praying, forgive, if
ye have ought against any: that your
Father also which is in heaven may forgive
you your trespasses. (Mark 11:25)**

Jesus told us to forgive the people who hurt us, and He said it in very strong terms. There are serious consequences if we fail to forgive. When He taught the disciples the Lord's Prayer, Jesus said:

And forgive us our debts, *as we forgive* our debtors.
(Matthew 6:12, emphasis added)

The Bible is very clear about this. We are to forgive others. Jesus emphasized this even further with the very first statement He made after teaching them the Lord's Prayer. He said:

For if ye forgive men their trespasses, your heavenly Father will also forgive you: But *if ye forgive not men their trespasses, neither will your Father forgive your trespasses.* (Matthew 6:14-15, emphasis added)

One of the Beatitudes relates to forgiveness. We need mercy from God. And we also need to be merciful to others. Jesus said:

> Blessed are the merciful: for they shall obtain mercy. (Matthew 5:7)

Do people who do nasty things deserve mercy? Of course not. They deserve Hell. But so do we. Every one of us is a sinner, and we all deserve to go to Hell. The only reason we can go to Heaven is because Jesus died for our sins. He was loving and merciful and forgiving with us when we did not deserve it at all. We need to follow the example of Jesus and show love and mercy to others:

> But God commendeth his love toward us, in that, while we were yet sinners, Christ died for us. (Romans 5:8)

Jesus told us we will reap what we sow. Therefore, if we sow mercy and forgiveness, then we will reap them. If we sow unforgiveness, then that is what we will reap:

> Be not deceived; God is not mocked: for whatsoever a man soweth, that shall he also reap. (Galatians 6:7)

Have you ever done any farming or gardening? One small seed can result in a large plant. I counted the number of grains on an ear of corn, and there were about 500 of them. If you planted one of those grains, you would get a plant with two or three ears of corn on it. That would be 1,000 to 1,500 times as many grains as you planted. This demonstrates that we need to be careful about what we sow, because we are going to get a lot of it back.

Sometimes it can be very difficult to forgive. In that case, we can ask God to make us willing to do it and to enable us to do it. He has told us in His Word that His grace is sufficient for us. That includes the grace to do difficult things like forgiving those who have done terrible things to us or to those we love. We can do whatever we need to do (including forgiving) because Jesus Christ will give us the strength to do it:

> And he said unto me, My grace is sufficient for thee: for my strength is made perfect in weakness. Most gladly therefore will I rather glory in my infirmities, that the power of Christ may rest upon me. (2 Corinthians 12:9)

Sometimes forgiving others is a gradual process that takes time, like working through the layers of an onion. You get through one layer and think you have gotten it done. And then you realize that you need to go deeper and forgive at a deeper level. If we have been seriously hurt, it may take a long time, even years. The important thing is to be moving in the right direction—to forgive as much as we are able to at the moment and ask God to enable us to do it more completely.

Corrie ten Boom and her sister Betsie were sent to a Nazi concentration camp because they hid Jews in their home. The guards were cruel, and they did some terrible things. Betsie was able to forgive them right away. She saw them as being like trapped, tormented animals, and she prayed for them. But it was different with Corrie. At first, she hated the guards, and she hated all Nazis. She had to keep praying and asking God to make her able to forgive. And finally, after a long struggle, she was able to do it.

Betsie died in that camp, but Corrie survived. After the war, she traveled the world, telling people about God's love and forgiveness. She even ministered to one of the guards and to a German nurse who had done something cruel to them in that camp.

On a practical note, forgiving somebody does not mean we trust them. If a person is harmful or dangerous, then we have to protect ourselves and our loved ones from them. What's more, *our* forgiving others doesn't mean they are pardoned. Only God can pardon. But God does not want us to hold bitterness in our hearts. Forgiving just means we are giving that person back to God, letting *Him* deal with that person, and handing over that heavy burden of hurt and bitterness to God rather than carrying it ourselves.

In some cases, we may not be able to tell the person we forgive them, because having any contact with them would be dangerous or unwise. But we can still forgive them, and we can pray for them. We can ask God to soften their hearts and open their eyes and bring them to salvation.

When Jesus sent the twelve apostles out to heal the sick and cast out demons, we have no record that they asked for more faith in order to be able to do it. They just went out and did it. However, when Jesus told them they had to keep on forgiving, they asked Him to increase their faith. They already had enough faith to do miracles, but forgiving was more difficult:

> Take heed to yourselves: If thy brother trespass against thee, rebuke him; and if he repent, forgive him. And if he trespass against thee seven times in a day, and seven times in a day turn again to thee, saying, I repent; thou shalt forgive him. And the apostles said unto the Lord, Increase our faith. (Luke 17:3-5)

Jesus told a very sobering parable about the importance of being merciful and forgiving. It talks about a servant who owed his master 10,000 talents. Most Bible scholars agree that was an enormous amount of money, equivalent today to at least hundreds of thousands of dollars. The parable also talks about another servant who owed money to the servant who had a huge debt. He owed 100 denarii, which is about three months' wages. That's a lot of money, but compared to 10,000 talents, it isn't much. Here is the parable:

> Therefore is the kingdom of heaven likened unto a certain king, which would take account of his servants. And when he had begun to reckon, one was brought unto him, which owed him ten thousand talents. But forasmuch as he had not to pay, his lord commanded him to be sold, and his

wife, and children, and all that he had, and payment to be made. The servant therefore fell down, and worshipped him, saying, Lord, have patience with me, and I will pay thee all. Then the lord of that servant was moved with compassion, and loosed him, and forgave him the debt.

But the same servant went out, and found one of his fellow-servants, which owed him an hundred pence: and he laid hands on him, and took him by the throat, saying, Pay me that thou owest. And his fellowservant fell down at his feet, and besought him, saying, Have patience with me, and I will pay thee all. And he would not: but went and cast him into prison, till he should pay the debt.

So when his fellowservants saw what was done, they were very sorry, and came and told unto their lord all that was done. Then his lord, after that he had called him, said unto him, O thou wicked servant, I forgave thee all that debt, because thou desiredst me: Shouldest not thou also have had compassion on thy fellowservant, even as I had pity on thee?

And his lord was wroth, and *delivered him to the tormentors,* till he should pay all that was due unto him. *So likewise shall my heavenly Father do also unto you, if ye from your hearts forgive not every one his brother their trespasses."* (Matthew 18:23-35, emphasis added)

The wicked servant was turned over to the "tormenters" until he paid the debt. But he would never be able to pay it. That debt was so large it would be extremely difficult (if not impossible) to pay it back even if the servant had a well-paying job. A man who is in prison can't earn much money, which means there was no way he could ever pay that debt. So in effect, the wicked servant was sentenced to being tortured for the rest of his life.

Have you ever noticed that bitter people who don't forgive are tormented people? Everything reminds them of their grievance, of the wrong done to them and the person (or people) who did it. That grievance becomes the center of their life. They become hard and harsh, and they wind up hurting other people because of their bad attitude.

The wrong done to them is not the source of their problem. The thing that causes them to be tormented is the state of their own heart.

There is an old saying that "The same sun that softens wax hardens clay."

We can see an example of that with Corrie and Betsie ten Boom. Even though they suffered greatly in the concentration camp and went through many traumatic experiences, the end result was they became sweeter and more loving. They helped many women in that camp come closer to God. Christian women were strengthened and encouraged, and some nonbelievers came to salvation. At the same time, I'm sure other women there became hard and bitter.

If we have a heart for God, and we are willing to do things His way (which includes forgiving), then there is absolutely nothing that can destroy us. It may cause us temporary suffering, but the end result will be getting closer to God and knowing Him better. In the end, we will be grateful we went through that experience because of the good fruit it bore in our lives. That good fruit is something we will enjoy for all eternity.

> Rejoice, and be exceeding glad: for great is your reward in heaven: for so persecuted they the prophets which were before you. (Matthew 5:12)

> Blessed is the man that endureth temptation: for when he is tried, he shall receive the crown of life, which the Lord hath promised to them that love him. (James 1:12)

> For I reckon that the sufferings of this present time are not worthy to be compared with the glory which shall be revealed in us. (Romans 8:18)

BLESSED IN THE CRUCIBLE
(by Frances Morrisson—my mother)

O be blessed, by our Creator:
The One who stretched out the heavens
by the breath of His mouth;
and declared out of nothingness LIGHT!
And all forms of LIFE!
the One who woos us beyond the
Curse and our resistance;
the One who gives each life a glorious purpose.

O Lord: You gave us hearts, and
breath, minds and limbs
to welcome, and be nourished, by Your Love and Word;
to seek Your Wisdom, strength and Ways;
to carry Faith in Hope, to Your gates of Justice:
washed in Your Love, strengthened by Your Mercy.

O Lord: How can we utter our praise high enough,
deep enough, with fullest joy in harmony?
How can we murmur our love beautifully enough?
How can we bask peacefully enough in Your Presence?
How can we spread Your message clearly enough?
But these we try, blessed in the crucible of living Life.

The integrity of the upright shall guide
them: but the perverseness of transgressors
shall destroy them. (Proverbs 11:3)

16
THE IMPORTANCE OF INTEGRITY

Recently I was talking with a friend, and she said, "These days, most people have no idea of the importance of integrity." Unfortunately, that is all too true. To show how much things have changed, when it came to business deals, my grandfather's handshake was worth more than a modern legal contract.

As Christians, we cannot afford to compromise our faith or biblical morality. The world is going to put us under a lot of pressure to do it. Therefore, we need to be determined ahead of time to stand our ground.

In the Navy, the term "integrity" means "water tight." In other words, a ship with no leaks.

We all know about the Titanic. After it hit the iceberg, it sank within a few hours. That collision created a huge leak, which was obviously disastrous. However, small leaks can also sink ships. It just takes longer. In addition, as water comes in through the leak, the pressure makes the hole get larger and larger. In other words, the leak incrementally gets bigger.

The world will pressure us to deny God in two ways. One method is by obvious, intense pressure. The other method is incrementally—one small step at a time, which makes it much more difficult to notice. Therefore, we have to be vigilant.

We need to keep our faith and our morality biblical and not allow them to become compromised. Not even in ways that seem to be small. The stakes are so high we cannot afford to compromise. This quote from the journals of the martyred missionary Jim Elliot makes a lot of sense:

> He is no fool who gives what he cannot keep to gain that which he cannot lose.

One area we need to guard is being truthful in our words and in our actions. We need to be men and women of truth. Our postmodern culture has become so permeated with lies and deception that people have become desensitized to it. However, God takes this very seriously:

> But the fearful, and unbelieving, and the abominable, and murderers, and whoremongers, and sorcerers, and idolaters, and *all liars,* shall have their part in the lake which burneth with fire and brimstone: which is the second death. (Revelation 21:8, emphasis added)

I think that by "fearful," it means people who allow fear to prevent them from following God and living according to His standards. We all feel fear at times. The point is, do we allow it to control our lives? Or do we turn to God for the strength and grace to do whatever we need to do, in spite of the fear?

As far as telling lies goes, there are some extreme occasions when godly people do it. For example, Corrie ten Boom and her family told lies in order to hide Jews in their home and protect them from being murdered by the Nazis. However, they hated having to tell lies, and they longed for the day when Hitler would be defeated by the Allies and such things would no longer be necessary.

We don't fully know our own hearts. In order to have integrity, we need to remember the words of David in the psalms:

Search me, O God, and know my heart: try me, and know
my thoughts: And see if there be any wicked way in me,
and lead me in the way everlasting. (Psalm 39:23-24)

What is the key to having integrity? Knowing, loving, and
obeying the Word of God. That will bring blessings to us and to
our children.

Thy word have I hid in mine heart, that I might not sin
against thee. (Psalm 119:11)

Thy word is a lamp unto my feet, and a light unto my
path. (Psalm 119:105)

Let integrity and uprightness preserve me; for I wait on
thee. (Psalm 25:21)

The just man walketh in his integrity: his children are
blessed after him. (Proverbs 20:7)

May God give us the strength, wisdom, and love to grow in
integrity and faithfulness to Him.

17

LOVING DIFFICULT PEOPLE

Jesus said the identifying mark of Christians should be their love. By "love," I mean biblical love, as opposed to what the world calls love. Biblical love involves the entire person, and it doesn't come and go with the ebb and flow of emotions. It involves discipline and commitment as opposed to being mushy. Jesus said:

By this shall all men know that ye are my disciples, if ye have love one to another. (John 13:35)

But I say unto you, Love your enemies, bless them that curse you, do good to them that hate you, and pray for them which despitefully use you, and persecute you; That ye may be the children of your Father which is in heaven: for he maketh his sun to rise on the evil and on the good, and sendeth rain on the just and on the unjust. (Matthew 5:44-45)

Love tells the truth, even when it is unpleasant. An example is when Nathan confronted King David with his sin. Of course, we can tell the truth gently rather than roughly. But even then, some things are difficult to hear. And they are often precisely what we most need to hear:

> Faithful are the wounds of a friend; but the kisses of an enemy are deceitful. (Proverbs 27:6)

love tells the truth, even when it is unpleasant

> But speaking the truth in love,
> may grow up into him in all things, which is the head,
> even Christ. (Ephesians 4:15)

Jesus loved us when we were rebellious sinners who deserved to go to Hell. He was willing to die for us precisely when we least deserved it:

> For when we were yet without strength, in due time Christ died for the ungodly. (Romans 5:6)

Why should we love difficult people? Because God told us to, and if He is truly our Lord, then we need to obey Him. But also, because Jesus loves them. We do it for His sake. Not because they deserve it, but because Jesus deserves it. We can be loving with difficult people for the sake of Jesus. He loves them so much He was willing to die for them. So we love them as a way of showing love for Jesus.

Some people are so nasty that the only way I can show them love is to pray for their salvation. But I can at least do that much, and it might make a difference. It's amazing what God can do.

God can reach some people who look like hopeless cases. For example, one of my Christian friends used to be a drug dealer and a satanist, and another used to be a member of Hells Angels. Both men have some problems because sin leaves scars. But they love the Lord, and they are trying to live biblically.

I heard the testimony of a man who had been a member of the Black Panthers before he became a Christian. He later became friends with a man who used to be a member of the KKK until God opened his eyes and changed his heart. A former Black Panther and a former KKK member are now brothers in Christ. We serve an awesome God!

We are limited in our ability to judge people. Sometimes we think they are good, when deep down inside they aren't. And sometimes we think they are hopelessly lost, but deep down inside, they are hungry for truth and looking for God.

The Bible says:

> [F]or the Lord seeth not as man seeth; for man looketh on the outward appearance, but the Lord looketh on the heart. (1 Samuel 16:7)

God can reach some people who look like hopeless cases

Remember the parable of the sower (Matthew 13:3-23). The seed was good, so the results of the sowing depended on the quality of the soil. Some soil looked good, but there were rocks underneath it, and the plants died as soon as there was hardship. Some soil looked good, but there were weed seeds in it, and the weeds overcame the plants. Some soil looked good, and it was, and the plants thrived and bore fruit.

Similarly, some people look good, but there is hardness under the surface, and the Word of God cannot bear fruit in their lives. Conversely, some people look hopelessly bad, but there is something in them that responds to the Word of God.

Like the sower in the parable, we should just sow love and leave the results to God. No matter how bad people are, we can at least pray for their salvation. And we can have mercy on them. God has been merciful to us, and He told us to be merciful to others:

> Be ye therefore merciful, as your Father also is merciful. (Luke 6:36)

If those people sin against us then we can do what Stephen did while he was being stoned and ask God not to hold that sin against them. God told us to forgive:

> And they stoned Stephen, calling upon God, and saying, Lord Jesus, receive my spirit. And he kneeled down, and cried with a loud voice, Lord, lay not this sin to their charge. And when he had said this, he fell asleep. (Acts 7:59-60)

Let us keep asking God to change our hearts and make us more loving, to let His love in us shine through to others.

Beloved, let us love one another: for love is of God; and every one that loveth is born of God, and knoweth God. He that loveth not knoweth not God; for God is love. (1 John 4:7-8)

As the Father hath loved me, so have I loved you: continue ye in my love. (John 15:9)

Oh the Deep Deep Love of Jesus
(by Samuel Frances, 1834-1925)

O the deep, deep love of Jesus,
Vast, unmeasured, boundless, free!
Rolling as a mighty ocean
In its fullness over me!
Underneath me, all around me,
Is the current of Thy love
Leading onward, leading homeward
To Thy glorious rest above!

O the deep, deep love of Jesus,
Spread His praise from shore to shore!
How He loveth, ever loveth,
Changeth never, nevermore!
How He watches o'er His loved ones,
Died to call them all His own;
How for them He intercedeth,
Watcheth o'er them from the throne!

O the deep, deep love of Jesus,
Love of every love the best!
'Tis an ocean vast of blessing,
'Tis a haven sweet of rest!
O the deep, deep love of Jesus,
'Tis a heaven of heavens to me;
And it lifts me up to glory,
For it lifts me up to Thee!

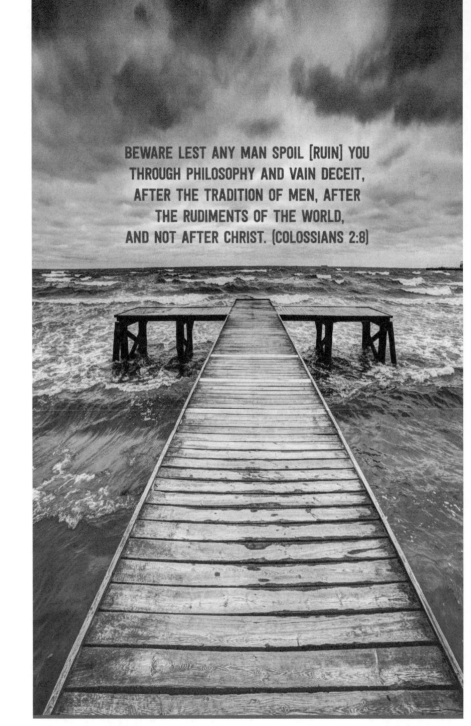

BEWARE LEST ANY MAN SPOIL [RUIN] YOU THROUGH PHILOSOPHY AND VAIN DECEIT, AFTER THE TRADITION OF MEN, AFTER THE RUDIMENTS OF THE WORLD, AND NOT AFTER CHRIST. (COLOSSIANS 2:8)

18

OVERCOMING HUMANIST BRAINWASHING

hapter one showed that for many years, humanists have been brainwashing kids in school and college with humanism, in an attempt to replace Christianity with the religion of humanism. And humanism is indeed a religion—an official tax-exempt religion in America. In addition, the entertainment industry and the media have been heavily promoting humanism for many years.

The very first statement in *The Humanist Manifesto* is, "Religious humanists regard the universe as self-existing and not created." The second statement is, "Humanism believes that man is a part of nature and that he has emerged as a result of a continuous process."[1]

Therefore, evolution is a core belief of humanism; it is the primary thing in their statement of faith. They have faith in evolution and utterly oppose the idea of creation.

The Bible speaks of God as Creator from Genesis to Revelation. If belief in God as Creator is undermined, then it becomes more difficult to trust God and believe the Bible. Humanist evolutionists recognize this and have openly stated it:

When the theory of evolution was advanced, that was the date that the Judeo-Christian religion began the decline in which it now finds itself in the West.[2]

Destroy Adam and Eve and original sin, and in the rubble you will find the sorry remains of the son of God.[3]

Darwin's discovery of the principle of evolution sounded the death knell of religious and moral values. It removed the ground from under the feet of traditional religion.[4]

Some evolutionists are quite open about their determination to believe in evolution for reasons having nothing to do with science. Harvard's Nobel Prize winning biologist George Wald said:

I do not want to believe in God. Therefore I choose to believe in that which I know is scientifically impossible, spontaneous generation leading to evolution.[5]

Some humanists and atheists have openly stated that Darwin's theory of evolution undermines Christian morality:

I suppose the reason we leaped at The Origins of Species was because the idea of God interfered with our sexual mores.[6]

By offering evolution in place of God as a cause of history, Darwin removed the theological basis of the moral code of Christendom.[7]

Many proclaiming Christians today believe in evolution or have tried to reinterpret Scripture in ways that fit with evolution. However, that weakens our faith, because from Genesis to the book of Revelation, the Bible clearly talks about God being our Creator. In addition, according to the Bible, death is the result of man's sin. But according to the theory of evolution, there were millions of years of death before man evolved.

Many years ago, I did an intense, in-depth study of this issue, and it made a huge difference in life. I had much more confidence in the Bible, and more trust in God.

I wrote a paper as I did my research. That is Appendix B, "Creation Versus Evolution." Please read it and also Appendix C which consists of Scripture quotations stating that God is our Creator. They come from many places in the Bible, beginning in Genesis and ending in Revelation.

There is another way in which humanism has been undermining Christianity—through humanistic psychology. This treats mental patients as being victims of circumstances or people with diseases—as opposed to being people who are responsible for their own behavior and who need to repent of their sins.

For example, "He's an alcoholic" sounds much like saying "He's a diabetic." The picture is that of a poor victim of some terrible disease. But if you say, "He's a drunkard," then that has a very different feel to it. The picture is a sinner who needs to repent and fight against his sin.

Psychology treats people as if they are driftwood rather than swimmers. Driftwood gets pulled along by every current that comes along. But swimmers decide where they are going to go, and they swim there in spite of the tug of currents. They fight the tug and head towards their goal.

There was an old Italian entertainer who said something along the following lines. I don't remember his name, and I don't remember the exact wording of what he said, but the basic idea was, "The neighborhood I grew up in was so tough that everybody who came out of that place wound up being a gangster or a policeman or a priest."

The point is, there are many different ways to react to the same circumstances. We can go with the trend, or we can fight against it. We can follow bad examples we grew up with, or we can be determined not to be like that, and by God's grace and strength, we can succeed.

For a number of years, I was a temporary secretary, working at a variety of companies. One of my assignments was working with a group of psychiatrists. I typed histories of their patients.

One patient was a man who was diagnosed with depression, low "self-esteem," and "mixed emotional features." When I read his history, I saw he had left his wife and children in order to shack up with an immoral young woman.

Well, a man who does that *should* have depression and low "self-esteem." That's not a mental problem. That's the Holy Spirit convicting him. The solution to the problem is not counseling and medication to help him get rid of his feelings of guilt. The solution is to confront him with his sin, help him repent, and tell him to make things right with his wife and children.

If people deal with sin—if they repent and forgive and try to live the way that the Bible tells us to live—then that will significantly reduce their mental problems. It may completely get rid of them. If not, then at least it will reduce them and make them easier to deal with.

For my thoughts are not your thoughts, neither are your ways my ways, saith the LORD. For as the heavens are higher than the earth, so are my ways higher than your ways, and my thoughts than your thoughts. (Isaiah 55:8-9)

19

THE BIG PICTURE—ETERNITY!

Looking unto Jesus the author and finisher of
our faith; who *for the joy that was set before
him* endured the cross, despising the shame,
and is set down at the right hand of the throne
of God. (Hebrews 12:2, emphasis added)

How was the apostle Paul able to endure great hardship
and suffering and yet call them a "light affliction"? He
was looking at the greatness of God and the glory of
eternity. He had some understanding of Heaven. He
had been "caught up to the third heaven," into "paradise," where
he heard amazing things he was not allowed to tell us about (2
Corinthians 12:2-4).

We need to focus on the really big picture—on Almighty God,
His amazing love for us, and on spending eternity with Him in
Heaven. If we do that, then we will be able to endure traumatic
things but still have peace and joy in spite of them:

> Thou wilt keep him in perfect peace, whose mind is
> stayed on thee: because he trusteth in thee. (Isaiah 26:3)

[T]he joy of the Lord is your strength. (Nehemiah 8:10)

We are not capable of comprehending how much God loves us, and the wonderful things He has prepared for us. The book of Revelation gives us a few brief glimpses of the joy in Heaven, but we won't really understand it until we get there.

God calls us children. Because they are young and lack experience, children don't understand the real value of things. They can shred paper money to use as nesting material for their pet gerbil, or draw pictures on the walls, or play catch with priceless china. Last year, a Ming Dynasty vase sold for over a million dollars, but a child wouldn't understand something like that. To him, it would just be another object to play with. It's similar to a puppy using your best shoes as a chew toy.

What God has waiting for us is far greater than we can possibly understand now.

> Nevertheless we, according to his promise, look for new heavens and a new earth, wherein dwelleth righteousness. (2 Peter 3:13)

> And God shall wipe away all tears from their eyes; and there shall be no more death, neither sorrow, nor crying, neither shall there be any more pain: for the former things are passed away. And he that sat upon the throne said, Behold, I make all things new. (Revelation 21:4 5)

But as it is written, Eye hath not seen, nor ear heard, neither have entered into the heart of man, the things which God hath prepared for them that love him. (1 Corinthians 2:9)

And they sing the song of Moses the servant of God, and the song of the Lamb, saying, Great and marvellous are thy works, Lord God Almighty; just and true are thy ways, thou King of saints. Who shall not fear thee, O Lord, and glorify thy name? for thou only art holy: for all nations shall come and worship before thee; for thy judgments are made manifest. (Revelation 15:3-4)

"Has a nation ever changed its gods? (Yet they are not gods at all.) But my people have exchanged their Glory for worthless idols. Be appalled at this, O heavens, and shudder with great horror," declares the LORD. "My people have committed two sins: They have forsaken me, the spring of living water, and have dug their own cisterns, broken cisterns that cannot hold water." (Jeremiah 2:11-13)

APPENDIX A

GODDESS WORSHIP IN AMERICA

The worship of pagan goddesses is most obvious with Wiccans. However, it is also common in universities and nursing schools. It is promoted by the media and is a component of New Age feminism. It has infiltrated mainline denominational churches and its influence can be felt throughout our society.

This movement is impacting our culture and especially the younger generation. One troubling aspect of it is that, according to some of its proponents, facts and logic are "patriarchal," and therefore they are irrelevant. As you will see, some so-called scholars openly say it is all right to make things up and present them as if they were historical facts.

Philip G. Davis is a professor of religious studies at the University of Prince Edward Island in Canada. He wrote the book *Goddess Unmasked* because he saw that goddess worship was being taken seriously in religious institutions and that myths about the goddess were being taught as factual history on campus. Most of the information in this appendix comes from his book.

Creating a Goddess-Friendly Culture

The "Age of Enlightenment" gave birth to rationalist materialism. In reaction against this denial of the importance of emotions, a generation of Romantic poets, novelists, artists, musicians and philosophers developed. Many of them were involved with drugs, the occult, Rosicrucianism, or Freemasonry.

Following Darwin's theory of evolution, they speculated wildly about the evolution of society. Nationalism became a romantic search for pagan roots, as seen in Wagner's operas and the fairy tales researched by the Brothers Grimm. Womanhood was idealized. The myth of a past utopian matriarchy was developed. Psychologist Carl Jung idealized the concept of the "anima," the feminine side of man.[1]

Romanticism even invaded history and archaeology. Bachoven developed a theory of matriarchy openly based on imagination and not on searching for hard facts. Feminist scholars followed Bachoven's lead. A historic myth was developed in which an ideal, matriarchal, goddess-worshipping society was destroyed by patriarchal invaders who brought with them all the ills of modern society.[2]

The scholarship involved in these studies of history and archaeology is so faulty that Philip Davis says:

> An important lesson of this book is the ease with which patent falsehoods may clothe themselves in the garb of scholarship and masquerade as truth.[3]

Feminist scholars and other academic radicals say objective facts and historical accuracy are not even a valid goal:

> A feminist scholar told her audience that it is indeed 'ethical' for an historian to ignore historical evidence in order to construct a narrative . . . while still presenting it as history.[4]

In addition to "constructing narratives" (i.e., making up stories and presenting it as history), many academic radicals "explicitly reject the quest for objective truth; they claim that objectivity is not only impossible to achieve in pure form, but actually illegitimate in the first place because it expresses a patriarchal, oppressive mentality."[5]

Before full-blown goddess worship developed in the 1950s, American art showed popular imagination being prepared for it. For example, the Statue of Liberty looks like a Greek goddess and is over three hundred feet high. The inscription presents the statue as speaking, and she calls herself "Mother of Exiles."[6] A 1915 poster for the Red Cross shows an American nurse with a billowing, hooded cape that makes her look like a cross between a nurse and a Greek goddess. She carries a placard which says:

> I am the Red Cross of Peace. I heal the wounds of war. I am a refuge from fire, flood and pestilence. The love of little children is mine.[7]

The National Academy of Sciences has a Great Hall done in Byzantine architecture designed to look like a "temple of science." The dome of that hall looks like it belongs in a cathedral, except it has figures that look like Greek goddesses. Science is personified as a goddess, with an inscription that says:

> To science, pilot of industry, conqueror of disease, multiplier of the harvest, explorer of the universe, revealer of nature's laws, eternal guide to truth.[8]

The Wiccan Goddess

Wicca was developed in England by Gerald B. Gardner, the first fully public witch of modern times. He was a spiritualist, a Freemason, and a Rosicrucian, with an extensive background in the occult.

Gardner was a member of the Golden Dawn. Aleister Crowley (a satanist) initiated Gardner into the fourth degree of the O.T.O. (Ordo Templi Orientis). Gardner was acquainted with a witch named "old Dorothy Fordham" and claimed to have been initiated into a coven. He used various occult texts in developing his rituals, including texts that were written by Aleister Crowley.[9]

Aiden Kelley, a Wiccan trained in biblical criticism, applied his critical skills to Gardner's archive. Based on Kelley's findings, Philip Davis concludes that:

> First, [Kelly's] identification of Gardner's literary sources leaves little doubt that Gardner's own witchcraft texts were his personal creation and not something handed on to him from an ancient tradition.[10]

Therefore, it is difficult to know how much Gardner's Wicca resembles ancient witchcraft.

Doreen Valiente was Gardner's High Priestess. She was informed enough to spot the passages from Crowley in the rituals, and she rewrote them so that Crowley's name would not discourage potential inquirers.

Initially, the male, horned god and the High Priest were preeminent. By the mid-1960s, the goddess was the supreme deity in Wicca, and ritual authority was vested in the High Priestess.[11]

Through Wicca, goddess worship has infiltrated our American culture:

> The appearance of the Goddess in other radical feminist circles, and then in churches and universities, did not occur until after the establishment of modern witchcraft as a viable new religion.[12]

> Goddess spirituality seems well on the way to becoming the most successful of all these neopagan manifestations in the English-speaking world.[13]

Wicca presents itself as a wholesome worship of a gentle, benevolent goddess. It's motto is, "An ye do none harm do what ye will." However, in real life the results of Wicca are not wholesome at all.

The Goddess and Mainline Churches

In November 1993, a Re-imagining Conference was held in Minneapolis. Most of the 2,000 participants were women.[14]

This was an ecumenical church conference attended by Presbyterians, Methodists, Lutherans, Roman Catholics, and members of almost a dozen other denominations. They invoked Sophia, the goddess of Wisdom, calling her their Creator. Prayers and liturgies were addressed to this goddess. Communion consisted of milk and honey instead of bread and wine.

They openly rejected the doctrines of the Incarnation and the Atonement. "Christian" lesbians were applauded for coming out of the closet. They encouraged "sex among friends" as a norm.

This conference was initiated by, sponsored by, and attended by representatives of the major American churches.[15]

> Re-imagining was an unprecedented event: an interdenominational assembly of Christians openly bent on destroying the historic Christian religion root and branch, and steering the churches into wholesale neopaganism.[16]

Neopagan and Wiccan themes are amazingly prominent within older religious establishments. One reason for this is the quest for "inclusive" language and the attempt to apply more female imagery to God. Liturgy reform and revised hymnals have featured feminine imagery and metaphors for God the Mother.[17]

The Unitarian-Universalist church developed a ten-session workshop on feminism, which encourages goddess worship and even endorses witchcraft. This workshop is called Cakes for the Queen of Heaven. It has been circulated through the major denominations and adopted for use in many mainstream churches.[18]

The following quotation from Jeremiah gives God's perspective about this:

> Do you not see what they are doing in the towns of Judah and in the streets of Jerusalem? The children gather wood,

173

> the fathers light the fire, and the women knead the dough and make *cakes of bread for the Queen of Heaven.* They pour out drink offerings to other gods to provoke me to anger. (Jeremiah 7:16-18, emphasis added)

A Canadian television station ran a five-part series titled *Return of the Goddess,* which introduced many people to goddess worship. The National Film Board of Canada produced *Goddess Remembered,* which became one of their most popular productions ever, being featured by public broadcasting TV stations in the United States as well as in Canada. *Cakes for the Queen of Heaven* and *Goddess Remembered* have both become staples for study groups in some major denominations.[19]

The Goddess and the University

The credibility of goddess worship has been increased by its acceptance by university professors and its incorporation into textbooks.[20]

> [T]he doctrines of a new religion are being packaged and promoted as factual material for use in publicly funded and accredited institutions of higher education.[21]

The broader plans of gender feminism seem to have been most fully articulated, promoted and implemented among academics. Some feminists have even demanded that the goddess be given parity with the God of the Bible in university religion programs. This will impact our entire society because universities and colleges are training most of our future leaders, including government, health care, and the clergy.[22]

> [R]adical professors are . . . using the classroom for recruitment, turning students into political activists. The campus, therefore, is a natural place to look for signs of the radical feminist New Age as it emerges.[23]

The Goddess and Health Care

Goddess worship has become strong in the field of health care, particularly nursing. Health care professionals are actively promoting New Age practices. For example, the occultic "therapeutic touch" (passing one's hands above a patient's body in order to manipulate auras and energy fields) has reportedly been taught to thousands of nurses in eighty North American nursing programs.[24]

Goddess worship has been overtly promoted, as can be seen from the following quotation from the National League for Nursing, which is an accrediting agency for nursing schools:

> Women's wisdom is ageless and timeless, and passes from generation to generation primarily by oral tradition. . . . These origins are grounded in women's experiences, female symbolism, and the spiritual roots of the Triple Goddess.[25]

What Can We Do?

We need to be informed so we can help people we know who have become confused by these things. God may show us practical things we can do. Above all, we need to take the following Scripture seriously, and apply it to our daily lives.

> If any of you lack wisdom, let him ask of God, that giveth to all men liberally, and upbraideth not; and it shall be given him. (James 1:5)

APPENDIX B

CREATION VERSUS EVOLUTION

Years ago, I was fighting cancer, and I needed to trust the Lord. In spite of the fact that God has always faithfully taken care of me, it was amazingly difficult for me to really trust Him. I said the right things and prayed the right prayers, but deep down inside, I was still afraid.

It is always easier to trust the Lord from a point of safety, but my difficulty went deeper than that. So for months I asked God to help me trust Him and to deal with whatever was hindering that trust.

Then, one day, someone unexpectedly gave me a catalog of books and videos produced by the Institute for Creation Research (ICR).[1]

Out of curiosity, I ordered a video on Mount Saint Helen's. On watching that video, I saw with my own eyes a wall of sediment six hundred feet high, which had been laid down by the volcano since 1980. Rather than being laid down gradually, it was laid down in spurts by lava flows, mud slides, etc. For example, in one day, 25 feet of finely stratified layers were laid down. Some of those layers were less than a centimeter thick, and were laid down in seconds. I had always been taught that layered rock like that takes millions of years to form.

I saw with my own eyes a 100-foot-deep canyon system carved out in one day by a hurricane-speed mud slide which cut through solid rock. The canyon system looked like a miniature Grand Canyon. It even had a stream running through the bottom of it. I had always been taught that canyon systems are formed over millions of years as a river gradually cuts its way down into the rock.

The video was interesting, but I had no idea how important it was until the next time I read the Bible. It seemed more real, more believable. I felt the Bible's authority in a way I had never felt it before.

I had always believed things I was personally familiar with. I believed Jesus healed people because I saw God heal my mother's back. I believed Jericho's walls fell down, and many other events in biblical history, because they have been verified by archaeologists. I believed biblical prophecy because it has been verified by history.[2] However, it was difficult for me to believe unfamiliar things such as Creation and Noah's flood. I was always looking for other evidence to support what Scripture said because the Bible's authority wasn't enough for me.

All my life, I've been interested in science. As a result, I was thoroughly steeped in evolution, both in school and through reading, TV, and movies. In college, my professors of religion taught me that the Genesis account of Creation isn't true because science has proved evolution, and therefore Genesis can't be taken to mean what it says. Starting with that assumption, they tore the entire Bible to pieces. And this happened in a college that claimed to be Christian!

Seeing the video on Mount Saint Helen's broke the power of what I had been taught in college. Evolution no longer seemed like a rock-hard, unquestionable fact. For the first time, I was free to seriously question evolution. For the first time, I was free to consider trusting the book of Genesis. The result was I found myself trusting the authority of the Bible in a new way.

I ordered more videos and some books. As I studied them, I saw a change take place in the way I shared the Gospel with people. Before, I had never been able to tell people why it was necessary for Jesus to shed His blood. I had heard and read the standard explanations many times, but they never really made sense to me. Intellectually, I knew that:

> For since by man came death, by man came also the resurrection of the dead. For as in Adam all die, even so in Christ shall all be made alive. (1 Corinthians 15:21-22)

I could quote it, but it didn't really make sense to me. However, once I became familiar with the creation books and videos, that statement came alive for me. For the first time in my Christian life, I became comfortable talking about the sin of Adam and the need for the shed blood of Jesus.

Before those creation materials set me free, I had been double minded. With part of my mind, I believed the Bible, and with part of my mind, I believed in evolution.

Evolution says that animals suffered and died for millions of years and gradually changed into people. In other words, death and suffering were in the world millions of years before Adam existed. The Bible says there was no death or suffering before Adam's sin. Therefore, evolution denies that death and suffering are the result of sin, thereby denying the reason that Jesus died. The following quotations from the *American Atheist* and *The Humanist* show the importance of this issue:

> When the theory of evolution was advanced, that was the date that the Judeo-Christian religion began the decline in which it now finds itself in the West.[3]

> Destroy Adam and Eve and original sin, and in the rubble you will find the sorry remains of the son of God.[4]

> Darwin's discovery of the principle of evolution sounded the death knell of religious and moral values. It removed the ground from under the feet of traditional religion.[5]

These quotations also show the importance of creation in evangelizing. It is difficult for people who believe in evolution to really believe the Bible, which means they usually aren't open to being led to Jesus through Scripture. Once people learn that creation is scientifically reasonable, then a major hindrance to faith is removed and they become more open to the Gospel. If you have never watched Roger Oakland's lecture series on creation versus evolution, *Searching for the Truth on Origins*, I would highly recommend it. Mr. Oakland explains how "creation evangelism" is a highly effective way to win people to Christ through showing them the evidence (which he provides in the series) that evolution is a faulty and unproven theory.

Two Opposing Religions

The controversy between creationism and evolution is not a disagreement between science and religion. Rather, it is a dispute between advocates of opposing religions: scientists who believe the Bible versus scientists who believe in humanism.

For humanists, evolution is one of their basic articles of faith. In America, humanism and atheism are both tax-exempt religions, as I explained earlier in this book.[6] Here is what some evolutionists have said:

> The fact that a theory so vague, so insufficiently verifiable, and so far from the criteria otherwise applied in "hard" science has become a dogma can only be explained on sociological grounds.[7]

> [The theory of evolution is] universally accepted not because it has been observed to occur or can be proved by logically coherent evidence to be true, but because the only alternative—special creation—is clearly incredible.[8]

> Many scientists who were formerly evolutionists have become creationists as a result of the scientific evidence. They have found that the scientific model of creation followed by a world-wide flood explains the evidence better than the scientific model of evolution.[9]

Scientific Problems with Evolution

There are many problems with the theory of evolution. For example, gradual improvements are supposed to be caused by mutations. However, geneticists say that mutations never cause beneficial changes—mutational changes are always harmful or neutral.

Chemicals are supposed to have formed simple life forms, but microbiologists have discovered there is no such thing as a simple life form. Even the most primitive one-celled creatures are incredibly complex. Scientists specializing in probability theory say:

> The chance that higher life forms might have emerged in this way is comparable with the chance that a tornado sweeping through a junk-yard might assemble a Boeing 747 from the materials therein.[10]

If evolution occurred, then the fossil record should be full of missing links. However, only a few have been found, and every single one of them is disputed by experts. For example, archaeopteryx used to be considered a missing link between reptiles and birds. However, fossils of modern birds have been found, which are older than archaeopteryx. (It can't have been a missing link—something slowly evolving into a bird—if birds already existed.) Also, the eohippus-to-horse transition has turned out to be a fallacy.

Every single ape man has turned out to be a regular human, a regular ape, or a fraud. Even the celebrated Lucy is considered by many experts to be a regular chimpanzee. The only bone in Lucy which makes her seem human is the knee joint, which was found a mile and a half away from the rest of the skeleton and 200 feet lower down in the rock. Skeletons of modern humans have been found which are older than any of the ape men. (Ape men can't have been slowly evolving into modern humans if modern humans already existed.)[11]

Evolutionists are so anxious to have evidence that ape men existed they continue to teach them in textbooks and museum exhibits long after they have been proved to be mistakes or frauds. For example,

Peking Man consisted of ape skulls, human implements, and the assumption that the owners of the skulls used the implements. However, six complete human skeletons were later found at the same site. Obviously, the humans were the creatures that used the human implements. In spite of that, Peking man continues to appear in textbooks and museum exhibits. Furthermore, a furnace was later found at the same site, along with a pile of ashes over two stories high. No primitive ape man could have built a furnace like that.

Java Man was a fraud, but it is still treated as an ape man. Eugene DuBois found an ape skull and a human leg bone and said they belonged to the same creature—an ape man. Before his death, DuBois confessed he had found two fully human skulls and four other human leg bones at the same site. Therefore, Java Man (also called Homo Erectus) was just a normal human. However, it is still presented as an ape man in textbooks and museum exhibits.

Piltdown Man was a deliberate fraud—a human skull cap and an ape's jaw with teeth that were filed down to look like human teeth. It had been chemically stained to look old. Piltdown Man was exhibited at the British Museum of Natural History in 1912.

Suppressing Evidence

In 1916, a dental anatomist examined Piltdown Man and wrote a report showing that it was a fake. However, the museum suppressed his report.[12] They exhibited a copy of the fossil, locked the original skull in a safe, and refused to allow scientists to examine it. Piltdown Man remained on exhibit until 1953. By then, the man who discovered the skull was no longer around. Personnel and policies at the museum had changed, and some scientists were allowed to date the skull. In the process, they discovered that it was a fraud.[13]

In other words, leading scientists of a world-renowned museum suppressed the information that Piltdown Man was a fraud. They exhibited Piltdown Man as an ape man for 41 years, even though they knew that it was a fake. Furthermore, they deliberately concealed the evidence by locking the fossil in a safe and refusing to let other scientists examine it. This shows a desperate need to convince people that ape men exist, whether or not there is any real evidence.

Suppression of evidence also takes the form of automatically discrediting any evidence which is contrary to evolutionary theory. I was always taught in Science class that if the facts don't fit your theory, you are supposed to change your theory—not throw out the facts. However, in practice, the opposite is often true.

Motives for suppressing evidence include job security, fear of causing a controversy, professional reputation, and the philosophical implications of evolution. Also, paleontologists don't get research grant money for finding apes or men; they only get it for finding ape men. Therefore, they are tempted to suppress evidence and claim that a find is an ape man when they know that it really isn't.

One example of suppressing evidence is the "Calavaras skull," which was found 130 feet below ground by a California gold miner. The skull was almost completely mineralized. It was authenticated by a physician as a modern type of skull. J.D. Whitney, chief of the California Geological Survey, authenticated that it was found in the Pliocene rock, which is supposed to be over two million years old.

The problem is that, according to the evolutionary timetable, human beings weren't around then. So it was assumed that the skull had been planted there—in spite of the fact that the rock was also full of stone mortars, bowls, and other signs of human workmanship. Also, how could anybody plant a skull in solid rock? To this day, the skull is ignored or explained away, while Whitney's report lies buried in the museum archives.[14]

Another example of suppressing evidence is two half-skeletons that were discovered in Utah in 1975. They were completely encased in rock. The bones were taken to the University of Utah for official testing and confirmation. However, nothing was done; no report was issued. The experts refused to follow up on this discovery. The man who discovered them had to come back to pick them up. Why were the experts afraid to follow up on it? Because the bones came out of a rock layer that was supposed to be a hundred million years old.[15]

Lack of Evidence

Fortunately, also, some evolutionists are scientists of integrity, men and women who genuinely seek the truth and aren't threatened by ideas different from what they were taught. Real truth-seekers aren't threatened by facts. They don't try to suppress evidence contrary to their position, and they don't try to exaggerate evidence that favors it. Such scientists are often aware of how shaky the evidence for evolution is in their own area of science, but, having been taught evolution by teachers they trust, they assume that other scientific disciplines must have the solid evidence for it. Once they study the evidence in other areas of science, and realize how weak it is, some of them become creationists.

Stephen Jay Gould, a prominent evolutionist from Harvard University, tried to explain the lack of fossil evidence by developing the theory of "punctuated equilibrium," which pictures evolutionary history as long periods when nothing happens, punctuated by sudden evolutionary spurts which occur so quickly that no record is left in the fossils. Other evolutionists have tried to explain the lack of solid evidence for evolution by saying that it occurred somewhere else in the universe and the resulting plants and animals were transported to Earth (the theory of "directed panspermia").

Many animals and plants show a precision of efficient engineering design that can't have occurred by chance. Some evolutionists recognize this but are unwilling to acknowledge that God is the designer. Therefore, they attribute plan and purpose to evolution itself, or to the earth, or to mystical New Age forces. In other words, they personify evolution (or the earth) and make a god out of it.

Michael Denton, an Australian microbiologist, believes in evolution and openly mocks the Genesis account of creation in his book *Evolution: A Theory in Crisis.*[16] Yet his book shows that biochemistry, microbiology, genetics, embryology, paleontology, and probability theory all fail to support the theory of evolution. His book contains so much information showing that the evidence of science is contrary to evolution that ICR scientists re-read it every time they are scheduled to have a public debate with evolutionists.

There is also the problem of how transitional forms could have survived. For example, according to the theory of evolution, reptiles gradually changed into birds, which means that their front legs gradually changed into wings over millions of years. But wings and legs function in completely different ways. How did those transitional animals survive without the use of their front legs during the millions of years before those legs became functional wings?

If you want to understand this in practical terms, then get down on the floor and crawl on all fours. While you are still crawling, suddenly pick up your arms and hold them out sideways like wings.

It takes more faith to believe in evolution than it does to believe in creation.

The problems of gradual evolution have led some scientists to postulate the "hopeful monster" theory, which says that one day a reptile laid an egg and a bird hatched from it. But a baby bird cannot survive without a mother bird to feed it, take care of it, and teach it to fly. No mother reptile could do that for a bird, even if she wanted to. (Reptiles lay their eggs and leave; they don't take care of their babies.) Also, how could such a bird reproduce with no other birds around? In spite of this, "hopeful monsters" are considered to be serious science, and articles about them are published in scientific journals. The American Association for the Advancement of Science even endorses a children's book which promotes the idea.

One of the world's greatest experts on fossils is Dr. Colin Patterson, Senior Paleontologist of the British Museum of Natural History. His museum contains over seven million fossils, which is the largest collection in the world. After more than twenty years of studying fossils, writing books on evolution, and teaching and speaking on evolution, he gave the following statement during his keynote address to prominent evolutionists at the American Museum of Natural History in New York City, on November 5, 1981. He said that, after studying evolution for twenty years, he realized that:

> [T]here was not one thing I knew about it. That's quite a shock to learn that one can be so misled so long.[17]

The introduction to the 1971 edition of Darwin's *The Origin of Species* states that evolution has not been scientifically proved, and therefore belief in evolution could be considered faith rather than science. It says that evolution is the foundation of biology and, as a result:

> [B]iology is thus in the peculiar position of being a science founded on an unproved theory—is it then a science or a faith?[18]

Harvard's Nobel Prize winning biologist George Wald said, in *Frontiers of Modern Biology on Theories of Origin of Life*:

> I do not want to believe in God. Therefore I choose to believe in that which I know is scientifically impossible, spontaneous generation leading to evolution.[19]

Problems with Dating

Evolution requires immense amounts of time to be at all plausible. (If a princess kisses a frog and it turns into a prince, that's a fairy tale. If a frog turns into a prince over millions of years, that's evolution.)

According to radiometric dating, the earth is over four billion years old. However, a number of problems with radiometric dating exist. It requires making several assumptions. Each one of these assumptions cannot be verified, and many scientists consider them to be unrealistic. Furthermore, as explained below, there is a problem caused by water.[20]

Radiometric dating depends on precise measurements of radioactive materials such as uranium, thorium, strontium, rubidium, and radioactive potassium. All of them occur as salts, which dissolve in water. If a rock containing them is left under water, the radioactive salts will leach out of the rock, and radiometric dating will show the rock to be far older than it really is. The presence of fossil fish on mountain tops indicates that the earth has known extensive flooding.

There are at least 68 other "natural clocks" which can be used to date the earth. These include:

- The rate at which land is washed into the ocean

- The rate at which salt collects in the ocean

- The amount of cosmic dust on the moon

- The decay of short-period comets

- The rate at which oil leaks out of oil deposits

- The earth's shrinking magnetic field

Most of these "clocks" give a maximum age of thousands of years.[21]

The inaccuracy of radiometric dating is shown by studies of underwater rocks which were formed less than 200 years ago by lava from two Hawaiian volcanoes (an active volcano named Kilauea and a volcano near Hualalai). The rocks were dated using radiometric dating. The ages obtained from Kilauea's rocks ranged up to 22 million years.[22] The ages obtained from rocks formed by the volcano near Hualalai ranged from 160 million years to three billion years.[23] Both sets of rocks are known to be less than 200 years old, because their formation by the volcanoes is a matter of historical record.

Evolutionist William Stansfield recognizes the serious problems with radiometric dating. In his textbook on evolution, he says:

> Age estimates on a given geological stratum using different methods are often quite different (sometimes by hundreds of millions of years).[24]

This is of great practical importance because, during Noah's flood, the entire earth was under water for over a year. The rain only lasted for forty days, but it remained twenty feet higher than the highest mountains for 150 days. After that, it took a year and ten days for the earth to dry out enough for Noah to come out of the ark (see Genesis 7:17-8:16).[25]

Many discoveries indicate that processes which we were taught take thousands or millions of years, actually occur quite quickly. For example, the volcano at Mount Saint Helen's laid down 25 feet of finely stratified layers in one day. Many of them were less than a centimeter thick and were laid down in seconds. A 100-foot-deep canyon system was carved out at Mount Saint Helen's in one day by a hurricane-speed mud slide which cut through solid rock. If you want to see these for yourself, get the video "Mount Saint Helen's" from ICR.

Other examples are coal and oil, which can be formed quite rapidly in a laboratory. They don't require millions of years. All they require is the right conditions.

Given the right conditions, wood can be petrified quickly and fossils can form quickly. Many fossils of modern items have been found, including a fossilized 20th century hat.

Many fossils have been found, which indicate rapid burial under catastrophic conditions. For example, a fossil of an eighty foot whale was found standing on its tail, buried in diatomaceous earth.[26] (Diatomaceous earth, or diatomite, is formed by microscopic organisms with hard exterior skeletons or shells.) That whale had to be buried so quickly that it couldn't rot or fall over. One witty letter to the editor in *Chemical & Engineering News* remarked:

> The baleen whale simply stood on its tail for 100,000 years, its skeleton undecomposing, while the diatomaceous snow covered its frame millimeter by millimeter.[27]

Conflicts with Laws of Science

Another basic problem with the theory of evolution is that it goes directly against several important laws of physical science. The Second Law of Thermodynamics, also known as the Law of Entropy, states that everything wears out, has less and less energy available for use, and becomes less and less ordered. You can see it all around you: your body is wearing out, your car gets more and more run down, you have to fight to maintain your house in decent shape. But evolution goes completely contrary to all that by saying that, on their own, things will become more and more complex, more ordered, that they will go upwards instead of running down. Evolution also goes contrary to the First Law of Thermodynamics (conservation of energy and matter). It also goes against the Law of Cause and Effect, and the Laws of Probability.

Humanist Agenda

Why is evolution taught so dogmatically as an absolute, unquestionable fact even though many scientists recognize there are serious difficulties with the theory? Because John Dewey (the "father of progressive education") almost singlehandedly revolutionized education in the United States. He was a staunch humanist and a signer of the original "Humanist Manifesto." He was determined to make the American school system conform to humanist ideals. An important part of that goal was indoctrinating students in evolution.[28]

The Bible says that one of the signs of the last days will be that people will choose to ignore three facts: (1) God created everything; (2) Noah's flood was a world-wide judgment sent by God; and (3) there will be a coming judgment by fire. The refusal to acknowledge these things will be associated with moral corruption:

> Knowing this first, that there shall come in the last days scoffers, walking after their own lusts, And saying, Where is the promise of his coming? For since the fathers fell asleep, all things continue as they were from the beginning of the creation. For this they willingly are ignorant of, that by the word of God the heavens were of old, and the earth standing out of the water and in the water: Whereby the world that then was, being overflowed with water, perished: But the heavens and the earth, which are now, by the same

word are kept in store, reserved unto fire against the day of judgment and perdition of ungodly men. (2 Peter 3:3-7)

Moral Consequences

There is a definite connection between moral corruption and not wanting to acknowledge God as our Creator. If God created us, then He makes the rules. If we evolved from animals, then we make the rules. Therefore, anybody who doesn't want to abide by God's rules has a vested interest in promoting evolution. Sir Julian Huxley, a famous atheist and one of the leading evolutionists of the 20th century, said during an interview on a talk show:

> I suppose the reason we leaped at *The Origin of Species* was because the idea of God interfered with our sexual mores.[29]

Widespread belief in evolution has had a devastating effect on the morals of our society. Even Will Durant, a humanist philosopher who doesn't believe he personally needs God, can recognize it:

> By offering evolution in place of God as a cause of history, Darwin removed the theological basis of the moral code of Christendom.[30]

The principles of biological evolution have been extended to social, economic and national affairs, with tragic consequences. These are extensively documented by Henry M. Morris (*The Long War Against God*) and Ian Taylor (*In the Minds of Men*).[31]

Hitler, Mussolini and Marx considered themselves to be applying the evolutionary principle of "survival of the fittest" to national affairs. Hitler believed that Jews were an inferior (less evolved) race. He decided to speed up the evolutionary process by exterminating them as part of his plan for producing a "super race" in Germany.

Slavery and racism were justified by saying that blacks have not evolved as far as whites. Evolutionary scientists publicly justified racism until Hitler's massacre of the Jews made it unpopular.

Another result of evolutionism was the murder of Australian Aborigines to provide specimens for study and museum exhibits. Some have estimated that as many as 10,000 dead bodies of Australia's Aborigines were shipped to British museums in an attempt to prove the widespread belief that they were the "missing link."[32]

Edward Ramsay, curator of the Australian Museum in Sydney in 1894, published a museum booklet which included Aborigines under the designation of "Australian Animals." It gave instructions on how to rob graves and how to plug up bullet wounds in freshly killed "specimens." "Collectors" working under Ramsay were paid bounties for Aborigine skulls, brains, skeletons, bodies, and skins for mounting.

Amalie Dietrich, a German evolutionist, was known as the "black angel of death" because she had so many Aborigines shot for specimens. In the United States, evolutionists also collected specimens of "subhumans." The Smithsonian Institution in Washington holds the remains of 15,000 individuals of various races. Even in quite modern times, aboriginal bones have been sought by major institutions. Aboriginal leaders and others are asking to have such remains be returned and given a decent burial.[33]

Evolution contributes to suicide, especially among teenagers. Physician Michael Girouard has, in the course of his medical practice, seen a marked increase in suicidal thoughts when teenagers in science classes accept what evolution says about them—that they are just animals who exist because of blind chance, with no reason for being.[34] A friend of mine vividly recalls the day in twelfth-grade science class when he suddenly saw the implications of evolution and concluded, "I'm just a piece of meat!"

Our nation was shocked by the brutal beating of Rodney King at the hands of the Los Angeles police. People were horrified by the events that followed: rioting, looting, burning, beatings, and killings. But should we really be surprised? What else would you expect from senseless animals? What we saw in Rodney King's beating, and in the riots that followed, is people living out the evolutionist philosophy they were taught in school.

School children are taught they are just animals who have evolved from apes. Many people say that our schools today are a zoo. But what else should we expect from children who were taught they are animals? Our teachers have been telling them they are animals, without thinking through what the practical consequences will be when they grow up.

Everybody knows that you can't have a watch without a watch-maker and you can't have an airplane without an engineer. But our school children are being taught that incredibly complex things, such as the eye and the human brain, developed by random chance. In other words, we have been teaching them to think illogically and to discount everything they have learned through personal experience about how things are made in the observable world around them. We have taught them to think the opposite of what logic, reason, and common sense teach them. Then should we be shocked to see them grow up to be people who do things that are illogical, unreasonable, and senseless?

Belief in evolution has had a devastating effect on our society. It has paved the way for widespread immorality, secular humanism, atheism, and New Age religions.[35]

The bad fruits of evolution are obvious, and Jesus said we would be able to recognize what things really are by their fruits (Matthew 7:17-20).

"Experts" Versus the Bible

The scientific case for creation is very strong. This is very encouraging. However, we must never depend on science to prove the Bible. Rather, we should let the Bible show us whether science is valid.

All human beings (including scientists) have limited knowledge, limited understanding, and questionable motives. They make mistakes, they deceive themselves, and sometimes they tell deliberate lies. We need to put our confidence in God, rather than in weak, fallible, sinful human beings.

God knows everything; there is no limit to His understanding, and He is absolutely truthful. This world will pass away, but "the word of our God shall stand forever" (Isaiah 40:8).

In the past, humanist "Bible scholars" told us that archaeology had disproved the Bible. But God raised up archaeologists to show that the Bible was right after all.

Humanists have told us that evolution is an undisputable scientific fact which disproves the Bible. But God has raised up scientists to show that creation explains the scientific evidence better than evolution does.

Humanism will continue to raise up "experts" in many fields who will try to disprove the Bible. And we will have to stand our ground and keep on trusting the Bible, whether or not those false claims are disproved in our lifetime. Jesus said:

> If ye abide in me, and my words abide in you, ye shall ask
> what ye will, and it shall be done unto you. (John 15:7)

The word "abide" can also be translated as "stand" and "endure." It is not a passive word. It has the military connotation of holding your ground against enemy attack. As Jesus said in the parable of the sower, the devil is always trying to snatch the Word of God out of our hearts. We need to stand our ground and refuse to let God's Word be stolen from us.

The Bible speaks of God as Creator from Genesis to Revelation. (See Appendix C, "Creation in Scripture.")

Creation is woven into the very fabric of Scripture. When Jesus was questioned about divorce, He used the creation account in Genesis as the basis for his response (Matthew 19:3-6). When the angel in the Book of Revelation flew in midair, proclaiming the "eternal gospel" to all mankind, he cried: "[W]orship him that made heaven, and earth, and the sea, and the fountains of waters" (Revelation 14:6-7).

Noah's Flood

Noah's Flood is also scriptural. The Institute for Creation Research (ICR) has many books and videos dealing with it. In addition, you can find information about it on their web site. (Information about ICR is given below.) I will just deal briefly with one aspect of the Flood.

Ethnology is the science of studying the writings of ancient ethnic groups of people. Historical records were available for thirty-three of these groups. These ethnic groups were located in widely separated areas, so they probably had little, if any, influence on one another. If a world-wide, catastrophic flood occurred, then we would expect many of these people groups to have some kind of record of it.

Examination of the writings of these thirty-three ethnic groups gives the following information. Every one of them mentions some type of flood. Ninety-four percent describe the flood as being totally destructive. Ninety-seven percent say that mankind was miraculously rescued from the flood. Eighty-five percent say that a boat was used to rescue mankind. Ninety-one percent say that animals were also saved. Seventy-six percent say that the boat landed on a mountain after the waters receded. Eighty-eight percent say that birds were sent forth from the boat to find out whether or not the flood waters had receded. Ninety-one percent mention divine favor being shown towards the survivors and refer to a "bow" [rainbow] of colors in the sky. Ninety-four percent say that after the destructive flood, the people who were saved offered public worship to a god.[36]

Sources of Information

- Institute for Creation Research (ICR), 1806 Royal Lane, Dallas, TX 75229 (phone 800-628-7640). ICR has books and videos at all levels from children's books to a technical journal. Most of their material is strictly scientific. Some of their scientific works also include a Christian perspective; www.ICR.org.

- Answers in Genesis, P.O. Box 510, Hebron, KY 41048 (phone

859-727-2222); www.answersingenesis.org.

• Films for Christ, 2628 West Birchwood Circle, Mesa, AZ 85202 (phone 800-FFC-2261). It is affiliated with Eden Communications, P.O. Box 41644, Mesa, AZ 85274 (phone 800 332 2261).

Recommended Books

• *What Is Creation Science?* by Henry M. Morris and Gary E. Parker. This is a good, general book on the creation-evolution controversy from a purely scientific perspective. Although it deals with a lot of technical material, it is readable and easy to understand.

• *In the Minds of Men* by Ian T. Taylor. This comprehensive book deals with the philosophy of evolution and the practical consequences of its influence on our society. It also presents important evidence against evolution which has been concealed from the general public.

• *Darwin on Trial* by Phillip E. Johnson. Johnson is a law professor who analyzes the case for evolution in terms of his legal specialty—logic and evidence. He exposes false reasoning, invalid evidence, and unscientific approaches, and he makes a strong case for evolution being a philosophy rather than a real science.

• *The Controversy: Roots of the Creation-Evolution Conflict* by Donald E. Chittick. This book deals with the worldview confrontation between the two belief systems of creation and evolution.

• *Not By Chance!* by Lee Spetner. Spetner is a recognized expert on the genetic code. He demonstrates conclusively that chance mutations will never result in evolutionary change. While not a Christian creationist, this Jewish scholar shows that all useful genetic information must have been present at the start.

• *Darwin's Black Box* by Michael Behe. Behe is a professor of biochemistry with expertise at the molecular level (cell level). He shows that Darwinism falls on its face at the molecular level. Nobody has even tried to deal with the irreducible complexity at the cellular level.

• *The Answers Book* by Ken Ham, Andrew Snelling, and Carl Wieland. This book scientifically addresses twelve of the most-asked questions on Genesis and the creation/evolution issue. (Available from ICR.)

• *The Genesis Flood* by John C. Whitcom and Henry M. Morris. This presents a thorough system for unifying and correlating scientific data on the earth's early history. It proposes a biblically based system of creationism and catastrophism. It is thoroughly documented. This book sparks dialogue and debate on Darwin and Jesus, science and the Bible, evolution and creation, culminating in what would later be called the birth of the modern creation science movement.

• *The Long War Against God* by Henry M. Morris. Millions of Christians have seen their faith diminished and left fragile by aggressive arguments for evolution, but few know the true story of a belief system that seeks to ultimately eliminate God. Dr. Morris reveals this compelling story, and reiterates the power of scriptural truth.

• *The Evolution Conspiracy* by Roger Oakland and Caryl Matrisciana (first released in 1991 by Harvest House; a new updated, expanded edition by Lighthouse Trails will be released in 2015). The book shows the occult and "religious" nature of evolution and how evolution has drastically affected our society.

• *Let There Be Light* by Roger Oakland, a biography. As a young man, Roger Oakland heads to university with the morals and values of his Christian parents intact. When he enters school, he believes in God as a Creator, but soon exchanges this for Darwinian evolution. After graduation, he begins teaching biology (with an emphasis on evolution) at the same university. Challenged one day by a young Christian student, Roger mocks the whole idea of Creation and God.

Recommended DVDs

- *God of Wonders*. This amazing documentary film takes us through the creation story and the Gospel with spectacular photography, and tremendous facts about God's marvelous handiwork in creation. Presented clearly, simply, and precisely by men of God—Dave Hunt, Roger Oakland, John Whitcomb, and others—are the wonderful attributes of God: His justice, His wisdom, His love (Produced by Eternal Productions, available through Lighthouse Trails).

- *Searching for the Truth on Origins*. A 14-part (four DVDs) lecture series by Roger Oakland filled with fascinating and convincing evidence for creation. Also discussion on "Creation Evangelism." Available through Lighthouse Trails.

- *The Wonders of God's Creation*. This 3-DVD set deals with the earth, animals, and mankind. Moody Bible Institute

- *Journeys to the Edge of Creation*. This 2-DVD set deals with astronomy. Moody Video

- *Origins*. This 6-DVD series features Dr. A. E. Wilder-Smith, an international speaker with three earned doctorates. These DVDs are beautiful, gracious, and persuasive. Although very scientific, they are not dry. Films for Christ, Marysville, WA

- *The World That Perished*. This DVD gives persuasive evidence for Noah's flood. It ends with a salvation message. Christian Answers

- *Mount Saint Helen's*. This DVD has dramatic photographs and film footage but the verbal presentation sounds like a college professor giving a lecture. Compel Media

APPENDIX C

CREATION IN SCRIPTURE

From Genesis to Revelation, the Bible speaks of God as our Creator. Here are some of those Scriptures:

In the beginning God created the heaven and the earth. (Genesis 1:1)

And God said, Let there be light: and there was light. And God saw the light, that it was good: and God divided the light from the darkness. And God called the light Day, and the darkness he called Night. And the evening and the morning were the first day. (Genesis 1:3-5)

And God said, Let us make man in our image, after our likeness: and let them have dominion over the fish of the sea, and over the fowl of the air, and over the cattle, and over all the earth, and over every creeping thing that creepeth upon the earth. So God created man in his own image, in the image of God created he him; male and female created he them. (Genesis 1:26-27)

And God saw every thing that he had made, and, behold, it was very good. (Genesis 1:31)

For in six days the Lord made heaven and earth, the sea, and all that in them is, and rested the seventh day: wherefore the Lord blessed the sabbath day, and hallowed it. (Exodus 20:11)

For ask now of the days that are past, which were before thee, since the day that God created man upon the earth. (Deuteronomy 4:32)

And Hezekiah prayed before the Lord, and said, O Lord God of Israel, which dwellest between the cherubims, thou art the God, even thou alone, of all the kingdoms of the earth; thou hast made heaven and earth. (2 Kings 19:15)

Thou, even thou, art Lord alone; thou hast made heaven, the heaven of heavens, with all their host, the earth, and all things that are therein, the seas, and all that is therein, and thou preservest them all; and the host of heaven worshipeth thee. (Nehemiah 9:6)

Thine hands have made me and fashioned me together round about. (Job 10:8)

In whose hand is the soul of every living thing, and the breath of all mankind. (Job 12:10)

He . . . hangeth the earth upon nothing. (Job 26:7)

[God said to Job:] Where wast thou when I laid the foundations of the earth? declare, if thou hast understanding. (Job 38:4)

When I consider thy heavens, the work of thy fingers, the moon and the stars, which thou hast ordained; What is man, that thou art mindful of him? And the son of man, that thou visitest him? (Psalm 8:3-4)

By the word of the Lord were the heavens made; and all the host of them by the breath of his mouth. (Psalm 33:6)

The heavens are thine, the earth also is thine: as for the world and the fulness thereof, thou has founded them. (Psalm 89:11)

Of old hast thou laid the foundation of the earth: and the heavens are the work of thy hands. (Psalm 102:25)

Bless the Lord, O my soul. O Lord my God, thou art very great; thou art clothed with honor and majesty. Who coverest thyself with light as with a garment: who stretchest out the heavens like a curtain . . . Who laid the foundations of the earth, that it should not be removed forever. (Psalm 104:1-2, 5)

Happy is he that hath the God of Jacob for his help, whose hope is in the Lord his God: Which made heaven, and earth, the sea, and all that therein is: which keepeth truth forever. (Psalm 146:5-6)

The Lord by wisdom hath founded the earth; by understanding hath he established the heavens. By his knowledge the depths are broken up, and the clouds drop down the dew. (Proverbs 3:19-20)

The hearing ear, and the seeing eye, the Lord hath made even both of them. (Proverbs 20:12)

[F]or shall the work say of him that made it, He made me not? Or shall the thing framed say of him that framed it, He had no understanding? (Isaiah 29:16)

Who hath measured the waters in the hollow of his hand, and meted out heaven with the span, and comprehended the dust of the earth in a measure, and weighed the mountains in scales, and the hills in a balance? (Isaiah 40:12)

Thus saith the Lord, thy redeemer, and he that formed thee from the womb, I am the Lord that maketh all things; that strecheth forth the heavens alone; that spreadeth abroad the earth by myself. (Isaiah 44:24)

I have made the earth, and created man upon it: I, even my hands, have stretched out the heavens, and all their host have I commanded. (Isaiah 45:12)

Mine hand also hath laid the foundation of the earth, and my right hand hath spanned the heavens. (Isaiah 48:13)

But now, O Lord, thou art our father; we are the clay, and thou our potter; and we all are the work of thy hand. (Isaiah 64:8)

He hath made the earth by his power, he hath established the world by his wisdom, and hath stretched out the heavens by his discretion. (Jeremiah 10:12)

I have made the earth, the man and the beast that are upon the ground, by my great power and by my outstretched arm, and have given it unto whom it seemed meet unto me. (Jeremiah 27:5)

Seek him that maketh the seven stars and orion. (Amos 5:8)

The burden of the word of the Lord for Israel, saith the Lord, which stretcheth forth the heavens, and layeth the foundation of the earth, and formeth the spirit of man within him. (Jeremiah 12:1)

Have we not all one father? Hath not one God created us? (Malachi 2:10)

In the beginning was the Word, and the Word was with God, and the Word was God. The same was in the beginning with God. All things were made by him; and without him was not any thing made that was made. (John 1:1-3)

He was in the world, and the world was made by him, and the world knew him not. (John 1:10)

And when they heard that, they lifted up their voice to God with one accord, and said, Lord, thou art God, which hast made heaven, and earth, and the sea, and all that in them is. (Acts 4:24)

God that made the world and all things therein, seeing that he is Lord of heaven and earth, dwelleth not in temples made with hands. (Acts 17:24)

For we are his workmanship, created in Christ Jesus unto good works, which God hath before ordained that we should walk in them. (Ephesians 2:10)

For by him were all things created, that are in heaven, and that are in earth, visible and invisible, whether they be thrones, or dominions, or principalities, or powers: all things were created by him, and for him. (Colossians 1:16)

God, who at sundry times and in divers manners spake in time past unto the fathers by the prophets, Hath in these last days spoken unto us by his Son, whom he hath appointed heir of all things, by whom also he made the worlds; Who being the brightness of his glory, and the express image of his person, and upholding all things by the word of his power, when he had by himself purged our sins, sat down on the right hand of the Majesty on high. (Hebrews 1:1-3)

For every house is builded by some man; but he that built all things is God. (Hebrews 3:4)

Through faith we understand that the worlds were framed by the word of God. (Hebrews 11:3)

Thou art worthy, O Lord, to receive glory and honor and power: for thou hast created all things, and for thy pleasure they are and were created. (Revelation 4:11)

Fear God, and give glory to him; for the hour of his judgment is come: and worship him that made heaven, and earth, and the sea, and the fountains of waters. (Revelation 14:7)

ENDNOTES

Chapter 1. Understanding the Times

1. G. Brock Chisholm, "The Re-Establishment of Peacetime Society" (*Psychiatry*, February 1946).

2. Ibid.

3. a. Arthur M. Jackson, "The Courts Define Humanism as a Religion." This article was published in *The Humanist Institute Quarterly*, Winter 1987; also see: www.arthurmjackson.com/rootsf.html

4. "Secular Humanists Give Dunphy Another Platform" (Eagle Forum, www.eagleforum.org/educate/1995/nov95/dunphy.html, citing John Dunphy, "A Religion for a New Age," *The Humanist*, January/February 1983).

5. Marriage and the Family, The British Humanist Association, 1969. Cited by Dr. Dennis L. Cuddy, *The Globalists* (Oklahoma City: Hearthstone Publishing, 2001), p. 124.

6. "Humanist Manifesto I" (This is the original Humanist Manifesto, written in 1933. Other versions have been written since then; http://americanhumanist.org/Humanism/Humanist_Manifesto_I).

7. Ian T. Taylor, *In the Minds of Men* (Toronto, ON: TFE Publishing, 1991, 3rd edition), p. 425.

8. Berit Kjos, *Brave New Schools* (Eugene, OR: Harvest House, 1995, from chapter 3: "A New Way of Thinking; www.crossroad.to/Books/BraveNewSchools/3-NewThinking.htm).

9. Thomas Sowell, "Indoctrinating the Children" (*Forbes,* February 1, 1993), p. 65.

10. Ibid.

11. G. Richard Bozarth, "On Keeping God Alive" (*American Atheist,* November 1977).

12. Dan Graves, "Yale Founded to Fight Liberalism" (www.christianity.com/church/church-history/timeline/1701-1800/yale-founded-to-fight-liberalism-11630185.html; also see: www.christianity.com/church/church-history/timeline/1701-1800/yale-founded-to-fight-liberalism-11630185.html).

13. Heather Clark, "Yale Students Receive Bestiality, Incest Sensitivity

Training During 'Sex Weekend'" (*Christian News Network*, March 10, 2013, http://christiannews.net/2013/03/10/yale-students-receive-bestiality-incest-sensitivity-training-during-sex-weekend; also see: Lee Moran, "What the Yale? Ivy League Students Admit to Bestiality, Desires about Incest, During 'Sex Weekend' Workshop" (*New York Daily News,* March 6, 2013, www.nydailynews.com/news/national/yale-students-admit-beatiality-sex-workshop-article-1.1280746).

14. "Most Twentysomethings Put Christianity on the Shelf Following Spiritually Active Teen Years" (September 11, 2006. www.barna.org/barna-update/article/16-teensnext-gen/147-most-twentysomethings-put-christianity-on-the-shelf-following-spiritually-active-teen-years); also see: "New Research Explores Teenage Views and Behavior Regarding the Supernatural" (January 23, 2006. www.barna.org/barna-update/article/5-barna-update/164-new-research-explores-teenage-views-and-behavior-regarding-the-supernatural).

15. "Pedophilia the Next 'Sexual-Rights' Revolution? Academica, psychologists expanding LGBT argument to 'minor-attracted persons'" (January 2, 2014. www.wnd.com/2014/01/pedophilia-the-next-sexual-rights-revolution).

16. Jose Martinez, "Nurse Sues Hospital Over Forced Abortion Assist" (*New York Daily News*, April 20, 2010, www.nydailynews.com/new-york/nurse-sues-hospital-forced-abortion-assist-article-1.448478); also see: Robert Knight, "Can the ACLU Force Catholic Hospitals to Perform Abortions?" December 5, 2013, www.washingtontimes.com/news/2013/dec/5/knight-treating-the-mother-by-killing-the-baby);

17. Heather Clark, "Supreme Court Sets Date for Hobby Lobby's Challenge to Obama's HHS Mandate" (January 12, 2014, http://christiannews.net/2014/01/12/supreme-court-sets-date-to-hear-hobby-lobbys-challenge-to-obamacare-abortion-pill-mandate).

18. Bob Unruh, "State 'Imposing' Its 'Gay' Beliefs on Cake Artist," January 7, 2014, www.wnd.com/2014/01/state-imposing-its-gay-beliefs-on-cake-artist); also see: Tony Perkins, "Judge to Colorado Baker: Bake Cakes For Gay 'Weddings' . . . Or Else" (December 10, 2013. www.lifesitenews.com/news/judge-to-colorado-baker-bake-a-cake-for-gay-weddings . . . or-else); also: "'Tolerance' Now Means Government-Coerced Celebration" (December 16, 2013, www.wnd.com/2013/12/tolerance-now-means-govt-coerced-celebration).

19. Todd Starnes, "NM Court Says Christian Photographers Must Compromise Beliefs' (*Fox News,* August 22, 2013, http://radio.fox-

news.com/toddstarnes/top-stories/nm-court-says-christian-photogra-phers-must-compromise-beliefs.html); Eric Schultze, "Religious Liberty and Gay Marriage Collide as New Mexico Photographer Loses Case" (http://www.deseretnews.com/article/765636407/New-Mexico-pho-tographer-loses-gay-marriage-case.html).

20. "Government Shutdown Results in Ban on Military Chaplains" (11/11/13, www.militarydefensefirm.com/Military-Criminal-Defense-Blog/2013/Octo-ber/Government-Shutdown-Results-in-Ban-on-Military-C.aspx).

21. Ken Klukowski, "Pentagon May Court Martial Soldiers Who Share Christian Faith" (*Breitbart*, May 1, 2013, www.breitbart.com/Big-Peace/2013/05/01/Breaking-Pentagon-Confirms-Will-Court-Mar-tial-Soldiers-Who-Share-Christian-Faith).

22. "A Clear and Present Danger: The Threat to Religious Liberty in the Military" (Family Research Council, March 21, 2014, http://down-loads.frc.org/EF/EF14C52.pdf).

23. Brent Baker, "Shooter's Anti-Christian Motive Missed & Not-ed" (Media Research Center, www.mediaresearch.org/cyberalerts/1999/cyb19990917.asp).

24. "Fort Worth Shootings: Tragedy at an Unarmed Church" (http://reformed-theology.org/html/issue10/hate_crime.htm).

25. Brent Baker, "Shooter's Anti-Christian Motive Missed & Noted, op. cit.; also see: "Do You Believe in God?" (WorldNetDaily, April 26, 1999, www.worldnetdaily.com/news/article.asp?ARTICLE_ID=14726).

Chapter 2. Brainwashing Christians?

1. Dave Bohon, "Baker Who Refused Same-Sex Couple Must Take Sensitivity Training" (*The New America,* June 6, 2014, www.the-newamerican.com/culture/faith-and-morals/item/18431-baker-who-refused-same-sex-couple-must-take-sensitivity-training).

2. Ibid.

3. Ibid.

4. Ibid.

5. Lee Duigon, "When the State Owns Your Soul" (News With Views, June 19, 2014, www.newswithviews.com/Duigon/lee256.htm).

6. Leslie Ford, "Government to Farmers: Host Same-Sex Wedding or Pay a $13,000 Fine" (*Daily Signal,* 8/19/14, http://dailysignal.com/2014/08/19/government-farmers-host-sex-wedding-pay-13000-fine; note: The most serious problem is not the fine. It is forcing them to take "re-education" classes in order to change their religious and moral

convictions. In other words, it is brainwashing and persecution.)

7. Todd Starnes, "Commission Says Christian Business Owners Should Leave Religion at Home" (Fox News, October 7, 2014, www.foxnews.com/opinion/2014/10/07/commissiion-says-christian-business-owners-shoud-leave-religion-at-home).

Chapter 3. Thought Police in Colleges

1. L. Ron Hubbard, "Propaganda by Redefinition of Words" (October 5, 1971; ciited in "Hubbard in His Own Words," www.xenu.net/archive/infopack/5.htm).

2. Bob Unruh, "University to Students: 'All Whites Are Racist.': Mandatory Program 'Treats' Politically Incorrect Attitudes" (WorldNetDaily, October 30, 2007, www.worldnetdaily.com/news/article.asp?ARTICLE_ID=58426).

3. Ibid.

4. Video: "Think What We Think . . . Or Else: Thought Control on the American Campus" (www.youtube.com/watch?v=6EbQfmVoOfM).

5. "William Wilberforce (1759-1833)" (www.brycchancarey.com/abolition/wilberforce.htm).

6. "James Reeb" (http://en.wikipedia.org/wiki/James_J._Reeb).

7. Bob Unruh, "University Drops 'Whites Are Racist' Plan: Prez Says: 'I have directed that the program be stopped immediately'" (WorldNetDaily, November 1, 2007, www.wnd.com/index.php?fa=PAGE.view&pageId=44340).

8. Bob Unruh, "'All Whites Racist' Indoctrination Revived!" (*WorldNetDaily*, May 28, 2008, www.wnd.com/index.php?fa=PAGE.printable&pageId=65532).

9. Bob Unruh "Teaching Plan: America 'an Oppressive Hellhole': University Outlines 'Re-education' for Those Who Hold 'Wrong' Views" (WorldNetDaily, November 27, 2009, www.wnd.com/index.php?fa=PAGE.printable&pageId=117313; also see: "Letter to University of Minnesota," www.crossroad.to/Quotes/Education/re-learning/letter-u-minnesota.htm).

10 Katherine Kerten, "At U, Future Teachers May Be Reeducated: They Must Denounce Exclusionary Biases and Embrace the Vision (Or else)" (*Star Tribune*, November 22, 2009, www.startribune.com/opinion/commentary/70662162.html).

Chapter 4. Teaching Kids to be Sociopaths

1. Colin Flaherty, "'Beach week' Draws Black Crowd—and Violence," WorldNetDaily, April 30, 2013, www.wnd.com/2013/04/beach

week draws black crowd and violence).

2. "Abortion Battles' Game Caught on Video" (www.youtube.com/watch?v=78rYupgxxoI).

3. "Teens Caught on Tape Laughing About Sexually Abusing and Urinating on Underage Girl" (www.youtube.com/watch?v=d9 JARpqoj4).

Chapter 5. A Biblical Warning for America

1. Catherine Edwards, "Wicca Infiltrates the Churches—Wiccan Rituals Gaining Popularity in Christian Churches" (Insight on the News, December 6, 1999, http://findarticles.com/p/articles/mi_m1571/is_45_15/ai_58050620).

2. Heather Clark, "Middle School Girls Forced to Ask Classmates for 'Lesbian Kiss' During Anti-Bullying Presentation" (Christian News Network, April 20, 2013, http://christiannews.net/2013/04/20/middle-school-girls-forced-to-ask-classmates-for-lesbian-kiss-during-anti-bullying-presentation).

3. "Two Kindergarten Five-Year-Olds Caught Having Sex in Bathroom" (Examiner, February 25, 2014, www.examiner.com/article/two-kindergarten-5-year-olds-caught-having sex-bathroom-teacher-may-be-fired).

4. Michael Snyder, "Sex and the Public Schools" (End of the American Dream, February 24, 2014, http://endoftheamericandream.com/archives/sex-and-the-public-schools).

5. Alyssa Farah, "Abortion's Toll of 55 Million Called 'Genocide,'" (WorldNetDaily, January 21, 2014. www.wnd.com/2014/01/abortions-toll-of-55-million-called-genocide).

6. Dr. Ginette Paris discusses her book *The Sacrament of Abortion* on her website. She is a psychologist, a therapist, and a professor at the Pacifica Institute in Santa Barbara, California. She is also a pagan. Her website includes sections on "pagan meditations" and "pagan grace": www.ginetteparis.com/psychologyofabortion/readexcerptonabortion.html.

7. Jerome R. Corsi, "Pedophilia the Next 'Sexual-Rights' Rebolution? Academia, Psychologists Expanding LGBT Argument to 'Minor-Attracted Persons'" (*WorldNetDaily*, January 2, 2014, www.wnd.com/2014/01/pedophilia-the-next-sexual-rights-revolution).

8. "New Research Explores Teenage Views and Behavior Regarding the Supernatural" (January 23, 200, www.barna.org/barna-update/article/5-barna-update/164-new-research-explores-teenage-views-and-behavior-regarding-the-supernatural).

9. Michael Snyder, "Sex and the Public Schools," op. cit.

10. Carl Teichrib, "Unveiling the Global Interfaith Agenda" (Kjos Min-

istries, October 2, 2011, www.crossroad.to/articles2/forcing change/11/ interfaith.htm).

11. To read more about Chrislam, read Mike Oppenheimer's article/ booklet titled, *Chrislam: The blending of Islam & Christianity:* http:// www.lighthousetrailsresearch.com/blog/?p=13109.

12. I found all of these attempts to mix Christianity with other religions by doing a quick search on the Internet. You can easily find them for yourself. Just search for "Christian" plus any other religion or spiritual practice that you can think of.

Chapter 6. Heading Toward Dictatorship
1. "Socialism vs. Freedom." (South Dakota Family Policy Council, www. sdfamily.org/Kitty+Wetrthmann, Video of a talk by Kitty Werthmann).

2. Sophie Castle-Clarke, "Adolf Hitler and Charismatic Leadership" (http://web.archive.org/web/20120430075716/http://sophie-castle-clarke. suite101.com/adolf-hitler-and-charmismatic-leadership-a63275).

3. To see a photo of Hitler with a little girl: www.fpp.co.uk/Hitler/ images/children/Inge_Terboven_on_Hitler.jpg and Hitler with a baby: www.golivewire.com/forums/img.cgi?i=62823.

4. Kitty Werthmann, "Don't Let Freedom Slip Away: Sobering Steps from Freedom to Fascism" (Kjos Ministries, www.crossroad.to/articles2/010/fascism.htm).

5. Tom DeWeese, "National ID: Another Step to Totalitarianism" (WorldNetDaily, www.wnd.com/index.php?fa=PAGE.printable&pageId=45536).

6. Lance Johnson, "Biometric National ID Card Could Be Mandated on All American Workers" (Natural News, March 28, 2013, www.naturalnews.com/039683_biometric_national_id_card_mandatory.html).

7. Donna Garner, "Cradle-to-Career Plan by Obama and Duncan" Kjos Ministries, www.crossroad.to/articles2/010/edwatch/garner/1-cradle-to-grave.htm).

8. Bob Unruh, "Court Orders Christian Child into Government Education: 10-Year-Old's 'Vigorous' Defense of Her Faith Condemned by Judge" (WorldNetDaily, www.wnd.com/index.php?fa=PAGE.printable&pageId=108084).

9.Dana Perino, "Where's the Outrage Over What Just Happened to Student Loans?" (Fox News, www.foxnews.com/opinion/2010/03/26/dana-perino-student-loans-health-care-sen-kent-conrad-democrats-students).

10. Bob Unruh, "Eye-Popping Power Grab: Licensing of U.S. Colleges: Federal Scheme Poses 'Greatest Threat to Academic Freedom in our Lifetime'" (WorldnetDaily, www.wnd.com/index.php?fa=PAGE.view&pageId=209589).

11. Jim Rutenberg and Bill Vlasic, "Chrysler Files to Seek Bankruptcy Protection" (New York Times, www.nytimes.com/2009/05/01/business/01auto.html).

12. Nick Zieminski, "Plan to Ax Dealers Not Chrysler's Decision" (Reuters, www.reuters.com/article/idUSN2632731920090526).

13. Edwin Black, "Eugenics and the Nazis—the California Connection"(SF Gate, www.waragainsttheweak.com/offSiteArchive/www.sfgate.com.

14. Kevin B. O'Reilly, "5 People Die under New Washington Physician-Assisted Suicide Law" (American Medical Association, www.ama-assn.org/amednews/2009/07/06/prsc0706.htm).

15. "Have Researched Euthanasia Speak Out" (Hospice Patients Alliance, www.hospicepatients.org/euth-experts-speak.html).

16. Kathleen Gilbert, "'The Weekend Cleanup: The Gruesome Aftermath of Legalized Euthanasia in Belgium" (http://www.euthanasia.com/belgium2009.html).

17. Betsy McCaughey, "Obama's Health Rationer-in-Chief: White House Health-Care Adviser Ezekiel Emanuel Blames the Hippocratic Oath for the 'Overuse' of Medical Care" (Wall Street Journal, http://www.wsj.com/articles/SB20001424052970203706604574374463280098676).

18. Peter J. Smith, "Palin Firestorm Brings Fresh Scrutiny to ObamaCare 'Death Panels'"(http://www.freerepublic.com/focus/f-news/2314081/posts?page=33).

19. John Lott, "Eric Holder: Gun Grabber" (Front Page Magazine, http://archive.frontpagemag.com/readArticle.aspx?ARTID=33694).

20. Greg Halvorson, "Obama, the U.N., and the Right to Bear Arms" (Canada Free Press, http://canadafreepress.com/index.php/article/18882).

21. Robert Spencer, "Obama Declares War on Free Speech" (Human Events, October 8, 2009, http://humanevents.com/2009/10/08/obama-declares-war-on-free-speech).

22. Jeff Poor, "FCC Commissioner: Return of Fairness Doctrine Could Control Web Content" (MRC Business, www.businessandmedia.org/printer/2008/20080812160747.aspx).

23. Matt Cover, "Inspired by Saul Alinsky, FCC 'Diversity' Chief Calls for 'Confrontational Movement' to Give Public Broadcasting Dominant Role in Communications" (CNS News, http://cnsnews.

com/news/article/inspired-saul-alinsky-fcc-diversity-chief-calls-con-frontational-movement-give-public).

24. Seton Motley, "FCC 'Diversity' Czar on Chavez's Venezuela: 'Incredible Democratic Revolution'" (MRC News, http://newsbusters.org/blogs/seton-motley/2009/08/28/video-fcc-diversity-czar-chavezs-venezuela-incredible-democratic-revol).

25. "Wave Goodbye to Internet Freedom: FCC Crosses the Rubicon into Online Regulation" (Washington Times, www.washingtontimes.com/news/2010/dec/2/wave-goodbye-to-internet-freedom).

26. Bruce Edward Walker, "FCC Commissioner Copps Proposes 'Public Value Test'" (The Heartland Institute, www.heartland.org/infotech-news.org/article/28940/FCC_Commissioner_Copps_Proposes_Public_Value_Test.html).

27. Ritt Goldstein, "US Planning to Recruit One in 24 Americans as Citizen Spies" (The Sydney Morning Herald, www.smh.com.au/articles/2002/07/14/1026185141232.html).

28. Berit Kjos, "Your Friendly Community Spies" (Kjos Ministries, www.crossroad.to/articles2/2002/spy.html).

29. Berit Kjos, "The War on Hate Bans Christian Values" (Kjos Ministries, www.crossroad.to/text/articles/cwhbcv3-98.html).

30. "Smartphone" (http://en.wikipedia.org/wiki/Smartphone).

31. Whitson Gordon, "How to Take Better Pictures with Your Smartphone's Camera" (http://lifehacker.com/5662812/how-to-take-better-pictures-with-your-smartphones-camera).

32. "iPhone" (http://en.wikipedia.org/wiki/IPhone).

33. Matt Liebowitz, "I Spy: Controversial PatriotApp Lets Citizens Alert the Feds" (Live Science, www.livescience.com/technology/patriot-app-iphone-101214.html).

34. Matt Liebowitz, "Controversial Patriot App. Lets Citizens Alert Feds" (NBC News, http://www.nbcnews.com/id/40666711/ns/technology_and_science-security/t/controversial-patriotapp-lets-citizens-alert-feds/#.VOawsyJAS00).

35. Jerome R. Corsi, "Bush Makes Power Grab" (WorldNetDaily, www.wnd.com/index.php?fa=PAGE.printable&pageId=41728).

36. Geoff Metcalf, "Hidden Threats—Part I" (WorldNetDaily, www.wnd.com/index.php?fa=PAGE.printable&pageId=6111).

37. Mark Anderson, "Concentration Camps in US: Are they Real?" (American Free Press, http://www.americanfreepress.net/html/hilder_concamps_7239.html).

38. Jerome R. Corsi, "North American Army Created without OK by Congress: U.S., Canada Ink Deal to Fight Domestic Emergencies" (WorldNetDaily, www.wnd.com/index.php?fa=PAGE.printable&pageId=57228).

39. Berit Kjos, "A UN Militia in Your Community?" (Kjos Minsitries, www.crossroad.to/text/articles/rapid-reaction99.htm).

40. Jerome R. Corsi, "Bill Creates Detention Camps in U.S. for 'Emergencies': Sweeping, Undefined Purpose Raises Worries about Military Police State" (WorldNet Daily, www.wnd.com/index.php?fa=PAGE.printable&pageId=87757).

41. Jim Kouri, "Is the US Government Preparing to Send Dissenters to Prison Camps?" (News With Views, www.newswithviews.com/NWV-News/news123.htm).

42. "Big Brother Loves 'Financial Reform'"(Washington Times, http://www.washingtontimes.com/news/2010/apr/30/big-brother-loves-financial-reform/).

43. "Financial Regulatory Windfall" (The American Spectator, http://spectator.org/articles/39662/financial-regulatory-windfall).

44. Bob Unruh, "New 'Safety Plan' Would Control What You Eat." (WorldNetDaily, www.wnd.com/index.php?fa=PAGE.printable&pageId=146957).

45. Bob Unruh, "Federal Agents Invade Farm for 5 a.m. Milk Inspection." (WorldNetDaily, http://www.wnd.com/2010/04/144557/).

46. Jeffrey Folks, "Future of the News."(American Thinker, July 16, 2010, www.americanthinker.com/2010/07/future_of_the_news.html).

47. "Obama's 'Big Brother' Vanishes from Speech: 'Civilian Security Force' Missing from 'Call to Service' Transcript" (WorldNetDaily, http://www.wnd.com/2008/07/69784).

48. "Civilian Security Force on Agenda Again" (WorldNetDaily, http://www.wnd.com/2009/03/92109/).

49. Chelsea Shilling, "Obamacare Prescription: 'Emergency Health Army'" (WorldNetDaily, www.wnd.com/index.php?fa=PAGE.view&pageId=132001).

50. Nancy Matthis, "Obama Just Got His Private Army" (http://web.archive.org/web/20110914131615/http://frontpage.americandaughter.com/?p=3549).

51. Chelsea Shilling, "Democrat: Let's Have Mandatory National Service" (WorldNetDaily, www.wnd.com/index.php?fa=PAGE.view&pageId=184325).

52. Rep. Rangel proposed this same bill in 2006 and 2007. Its provi-

sions are discussed in "The Draft is Back—Again! 'Universal National Service Act of 2006'" by Berit Kjos at www.crossroad.to/articles2/006/draft.htm.

53. "National Security Letter" (http://en.wikipedia.org/wiki/National_Security_Letter).

54. Judge Andrew Napolitano, Natural Rights Patriot Act—Part 3 of 3, www.youtube.com/watch_popup?v=7n2m-X7OIuY; (Note: The information begins at 2:01 minutes, starting with the sentence, "Do you know that the Congress has used the Commerce Clause to make it a crime for you to speak the truth?").

55. Charles Krauthammer, "Government by Regulation" (National Review, December 31, 2010, http://web.archive.org/web/20110104035516/http://www.nationalreview.com/articles/256104/government-regulation-charles-krauthammer?).

56. Juliet Eilperin, "White House Presses for New Climate, Wilderness Protections" (The Washington Post, December 24, 2010. www.washingtonpost.com/wp-dyn/content/article/2010/12/23/AR2010122305643.html).

57. Cliff Kincaid, "Media Excuse Obama's Power Grab" (Accuracy in Media, December 26, 2010, http://www.aim.org/aim-column/media-excuse-obama%e2%80%99s-power-grab).

58. Sarah Rosen Wartell and John Podesta, "The Power of the President: Recommendations to Advance Progressive Change" (Center for American Progress, November 16, 2010, https://www.americanprogress.org/issues/open-government/report/2010/11/16/8658/the-power-of-the-president/).

59. Associated Press, "Medicare Regulation Revives End-of-Life Planning" (USA Today, December 25, 2010. http://usatoday30.usatoday.com/news/washington/2010-12-26-medicare_N.htm).

60. Charles Krauthammer, "Government by Regulation," op., cit.

61. "SWAT Team conducts food raid in rural Ohio" (Kjos Ministries, www.crossroad.to/articles2/08/swat-team.htm).

Chapter 7. Mainstreaming Occultism

1. Catherine Edwards, "Wicca Infiltrates the Churches" (*Insight Magazine Online*, Vol. 15, No. 45, December 6, 1999; can read at: http://www.confessingumc.org/news-events/wicca-infiltrates-the-churches).

2. Sarah Netter, "Satanist Church Rents Out Oklahoma City Civic Center for Exorcism" (ABC News, September 1, 2010, http://abcnews.go.com/US/satanist-church-rents-oklahoma-civic-center-exorcism-ritu-

al/story?id=11524098; this article is two pages. The link below goes to the first one, which leads to the second).

3. Daniel Lovering, "Plans for 'Black Mass' at Harvard Anger Boston Catholics" (Reuters, May 9, 2014, www.reuters.com/article/2014/05/09/us-usa-harvard-satanists-idUSBREA-48OOD20140509); also see: Travis Andersen and Derek J. Anderson, "Amid Outcry, Black Mass at Harvard Is Called Off," (Boston Globe, May 13, 2014.http://www.bostonglobe.com/metro/2014/05/12/cardinal-sean-malley-expresses-disappointment-harvard-decision-allow-black-mass-campus/tUjYx2817C65LAHousRIeP/story.html).

4. Brownie Marie, "Satanic Black Mass Coming to Oklahoma Civic Center" (Christian Today, July 30, 2014, www.christiantoday.com/article/satanic.black.mass.coming.oklahoma.civic.center/39180.htm).

5. Associated Press, "Devil-Worship Group Unveils Satanic Statue Design for Oklahoma State Capitol," (New York Daily News, January 7, 2014, www.nydailynews.com/news/politics/devil-worship-group-unveils-satanic-statue-design-oklahoma-state-capitol-article-1.1568893).

6. Berit Kjos, "Deceived by a Counterfeit 'Jesus': The Twisted 'Truths' of The Shack and A Course in Miracles" (Kjos Ministries, www.crossroad.to/articles2/08/shack.htm).

7. "The Clergy Project" (www.clergyproject.org).

8. "Dark Horse" (Katy Perry Song) (http://en.wikipedia.org/wiki/Dark_Horse_(Katy_Perry_song)); also see: "Katy Perry & Juicy J Are Fiery Satanists As They Perform 'Dark Horse' At The 2014 Grammys!" (Perez Hilton, January 26, 2014, http:perezhilton.com/2014-01-26-grammys-2014-katy-perry-performs-dark-horse-juicy-j).

Chapter 8. Dealing with Shock

1.Ken Klukowski, "Baker Faces Prison for Refusing to Bake Same-Sex Wedding Cake" (Breitbart, December 12, 2013.www.breitbart.com/Big-Government/2013/12/12/Christian-Baker-Willing-To-Go-to-Jail-for-Declining-Gay-Wedding-Cake).

Chapter 9. Fighting Fear

1. Jack Minor, "Military Warned 'Evangelicals' No. 1 Threat: Christians Targeted Ahead of Muslim Brotherhood, Al-Quaida, KKK" (WorldNetDaily, April 5, 2013, www.wnd.com/2014/04/military-warned-evangelicals-no-1-threat); Steve Ahle, "Colorado State Police and Homeland Security Target Christians As Anti-Patriots" (April

6, 2013, http://beforeitsnews.com/economics-and-politics/2013/04/
breaking-news-colorado-state-police-and-homeland-security-tar-
get-christians-as-anti-patriots-2451594.html); Leigh Jones, "Army
Reserve Presentation Calls Christians 'Extremists'" (World Magazine,
April 5, 2013, www.worldmag.com/2013/04/army_reserve_presen-
tation_calls_christians_extremists); "Pro-Lifers Should Be Concerned
About Obama Assassination List: Judge Napolitano" (February 6, 2013,
Life Site News, www.lifesitenews.com/news/will-pro-life-errorists-be-
names-to-obamas-assassination-list); Michael Snyder, "72 Types Of
Americans That Are Considered 'Potential Terrorists' In Official Government Documents" (The Truth, August 26, 2013.http://thetruth-
wins.com/archives/72-types-of-americans-that-are-considered-poten-
tial-terrorists-in-official-government-documents).

Chapter 10. The Bottom Line
1. The Clergy Project is an online support group for pastors who are
atheists. Their motto is "Moving beyond faith"(www.clergyproject.org).

Chapter 11. Building Faith
1. Sir William Ramsay, *The Bearing of Recent Discovery on the Trust-
worthiness of the New Testament* (Hodder & Stoughton, 1915), p. 85.
2. Ibid., p. 89.
3. Ibid., p. 222.
4. Ibid.
5. Harry A. Ironside, in the public domain.

Chapter 13. Don't Give the Devil a Beachhead
1. In 1981, John Keating published a book titled *Strength Under Control: Meekness and Zeal.*

Chapter 14. Giving Thanks to God
1. G. Richard Bozarth, "On Keeping God Alive" (*American Atheist,*
November 1977). In this article, he said: "We must ask how we can kill
the God of Christianity."
2. "Baker Faces Prison for Refusing to Bake Same-Sex Wedding
Cake," op. cit.

Chapter 18. Overcoming Humanist Brainwashing
1. *Humanist Manifesto I* (http://americanhumanist.org/Humanism/

Humanist_Manifesto_I. This is the original Humanist Manifesto written in 1933. Other versions have been written since then.).

2. O. Hambling, "Genesis and Evolution" (*American Atheist,* January 1988), p. 7; quoted in Henry M. Morris, *The Long War Against God* (Grand Rapids, MI: Baker Book House, 1989), p. 119; available from ICR.

3. G. Richard Bozarth, "The Meaning of Evolution" (*American Atheist,* February 1978), p. 30; quoted in *The Long War Against God,* op. cit. p. 119.

4. S. S. Chawla, "A Philosophical Journey to the West" (*The Humanist,* Vol. 24, September/October, 1964), p. 151, cited in Ian T. Taylor*, In the Minds of Men* (Toronto, ON: 1991, 3ʳᵈ edition), p. 422.

5. George Wald, *Frontiers of Modern Biology on Theories of Origin of Life* (New York: Houghton Mifflin, 1972) p. 187, quoted in Rex Russell, M.D., *What the Bible Says About Healthy Living* (Ventura, CA: Regal Books), pp. 273-274.

6. Quoted by Henry M. Morris, *The Troubled Waters of Evolution* (San Diego: Creation-Life Publishers, 1974), p. 58; available from ICR.

7. Will Durant, "Are We in the Last Stage of a Pagan Period?" (Chicago Tribune, April 1980); quoted in Henry M. Morris, *The Long War Against God,* op. cit., p. 149.

Appendix A. Goddess Worship in America

1. Philip G. Davis, *Goddess Unmasked: The Rise of Neopagan Feminist Spirituality* (Dallas, TX: Spence Publishing Company, 1999), chapters 2 through 12.

2. Ibid., chapters 2, 11 and 12.

3. Ibid., p. ix.

4. Ibid., p. 360.

5. Ibid.

6. Information obtained by phone from the Public Information Office of the Statue of Liberty.

7. This poster is in the Valentine Museum in Richmond, Virginia. A picture of it appeared in the Richmond Times-Dispatch, September 29, 1998, p. D-1.

8. The National Academy of Sciences—The Main Foyer and the Great Hall: This says that the architecht wanted to create a "temple of science," www.nasonline.org/about-nas/visiting/nas/nas-building/the-main-foyer-and-the-great.html; The Great Hall: This shows pictures of some of the goddesses. You can see that the ceiling looks like a cathedral rath-

er than a science building, www.nasonline.org/about-nas/visiting-nas/nas-building/the-great-hall.html.

9. Philip G. Davis, *Goddess Unmasked: The Rise of Neopagan Feminist Spirituality*, op. cit., p. 334.

10. Ibid.

11. Ibid., pp. 336-337.

12. Ibid., p. 341.

13. Ibid., p. 343.

14. http://en.wikipedia.org/wiki/Re-Imagining_(Christian_feminist_conference).

15. Philip G. Davis, *Goddess Unmasked: The Rise of Neopagan Feminist Spirituality* op. cit., pp. 3-4, 28-29.

16. Ibid., p. 29.

17. Ibid., pp. 24-25, 27.

18. Ibid., pp. 24-25.

19. Ibid., pp. 25-27.

20. Ibid., pp. 29-31.

21. Ibid., p. 31.

22. Ibid., pp. 361, 363.

23. Ibid., p. 361.

24. Ibid., pp. 31-33.

25. Charlene E. Wheeler and Peggy L. Chinn, *Peace and Power: A Handbook of Feminist Process* (New York, NY: National League for Nursing, 3rd edition), pp. xi-xii. Quoted in *Goddess Unmasked*, p. 32.

26. "Halloween: Its Origins and Customs" (www.jeremiahproject.com/halloween.txt.

Appendix B. Creation Versus Evolution

1. The Institute for Creation Research (ICR), 1806 Royal Lane, Dallas, TX 75229 (phone 800-628-7640). They have children's books, home schooling materials, books and videos for laymen, *Creation Magazine*, technical monographs, and a technical journal. They also have speakers available for presentations, debates, and Christian media. Their website is www.ICR.org.

2. See Josh McDowell, *Evidence That Demands a Verdict*, Vol. I (1979) and Vol. II (1990) (San Bernardino, CA: Here's Life). Fulfilled prophecy is discussed in pages 267-324 of Volume I. Archeological discoveries relating to biblical history are discussed in pages 17-24 of Volume II.

3. O. Hambling, "Genesis and Evolution," op. cit., p. 7; quoted in

Henry M. Morris, *The Long War Against God,* op. cit., p. 119; available from ICR.

4. G. Richard Bozarth, "The Meaning of Evolution," op. cit., p. 30; quoted in *The Long War Against God,* op. cit., p. 119.

5. S. S. Chawla, "A Philosophical Journey to the West," op. cit., p. 151; cited in Ian T. Taylor, *In the Minds of Men,* op. cit., p. 422.

6. Ian T. Taylor, *In the Minds of Men,* op. cit., pp. 394-395 and 420-422.

7. Biologist Ludwig Von Bertalanffy, as quoted by Huston Smith, *Beyond the Post-Modern Mind* (New York: Crossroads, 1982), p. 173; quoted in *The Illustrated Origins Answer Book* (P.O. Box 41644, Mesa, AZ: Eden Productions, 1991), p. 114.

8. D. M. S. Watson, "Adaptation" (*Nature,* Vol. 123, 1929), p. 233; quoted in Henry M. Morris, *Scientific Creationism* (El Cajon, CA: Master Books, 2nd edition, 1985), p. 8.

9. Luther D. Sunderland, *Darwin's Enigma: Fossils and Other Problems* (Santee, CA: Master Books, 1988, 4th edition), pp. 7-8.

10. Sir Fred Hoyle, "Hoyle on Evolution" (*Nature,* November 12, 1981, Vol. 294), p. 105; quoted in *The Revised Quote Book* (Sunnybank, Brisbane, Australia: Creation Science Foundation Ltd., 1990), p. 21.

11. See *In the Minds of Men* by Ian Taylor. Point by point, it exposes the fuzzy reasoning behind textbook presentations of evolution. It also presents counter-evidence that has long been concealed from the general public.

12. Peking Man, Java Man, Piltdown Man, and all of the other "ape men" turned out to be normal men, normal apes, or frauds. Revealing evidence about them is shown in the video "Ape Men: Monkey Business Falsely Called Science," which is available from ICR.

13. Phillip E. Johnson, *Darwin on Trial* (Downers Grove, IL: Intervarsity Press, 1991), p. 187. This outstanding book was written by a law professor who specializes in logic and evidence.

14. Ian T. Taylor, *In the Minds of Men*, op. cit., pp. 217-218.

15. Dennis R. Petersen, *Unlocking the Mysteries of Creation* (El Dorado, CA: Creation Resource Foundation, 1988) p. 131.

16. Michael Denton, *Evolution: A Theory in Crisis* (Bethesda, MD: Adler & Adler, Publishers, Inc., 1985).

17. This speech was tape recorded and transcribed with the permission of Dr. Patterson, quoted in *The Revised Quote Book*, op. cit., p. 4.

18. L. Harrison Matthews, FRS, *Introduction to Darwin's The Origin*

of Species (London: J. M. Dent & Sons. Ltd., 1971), p. xi; quoted in The *Revised Quote Book*, op. cit., p. 2.

19. George Wald, *Frontiers of Modern Biology on Theories of Origin of Life* (New York, NY: Houghton Mifflin, 1972) p. 187; quoted in Rex Russell, M.D., *What the Bible Says About Healthy Living* (Ventura, CA: Regal Books), pp. 273-274.

20. See Henry M. Morris, editor, *Scientific Creationism* (El Cajon, CA: Master Books, 1985, 2nd edition), pp. 131-170; also see Henry M. Morris and Gary E. Parker, *What Is Creation Science?* (El Cajon, CA: Master Books, 1987), pp. 253-293. Also see the video "Evolution: Fact or Belief?" These are all available from ICR.

21. Henry M. Morris and Gary E. Parker, *What Is Creation Science?*, op. cit., pp. 284-293.

22. C.S. Noble and J.J. Naughton, "Deep-Ocean Basalts: Inert Gas Content and Uncertainties in Age Dating" (*Science,* October 11, 1968, Vol. 162), p. 265; cited in *Scientific Creationism*, op. cit., pp 146-147.

23. J.G. Funkhouser and J.J. Naughton (Journal of Geophysical Research, July 15, 1968, Vol. 73), p. 4606; cited in *Scientific Creationism*, op. cit., p. 147.

24. William D. Stansfield, *The Science of Evolution* (New York: Mac-Millan, 1977) p. 84, see pp. 80-84; quoted in *What Is Creation Science?* op. cit., p. 285.

25. The flood began on the 17th day of the second month of the year. (Genesis 7:11). On the 7th month, the ark landed on Mount Ararat (the highest mountain) (Genesis 8:3-4). On the 10th month, the water had gone down enough for the tops of other mountains to become visible (Genesis 8:5). On the 27th day of the second month of the following year (one year and ten days after the flood started), God told Noah to come out of the ark (Genesis 8:13-15).

26. Kenneth M. Reese, "Newscripts" (*Chemical & Engineering News,* October 11, 1976), page 40; cited in Donald E. Chittick, *The Controversy: Roots of the Creation-Evolution Conflict* (Portland, OR: Multnomah Press, 1984), pp. 218-219.

27. Harvey O. Olney III, "Letters" (*Chemical & Engineering News,* January 24, 1977), p 5; cited in Donald E. Chittick, *The Controversy: Roots of the Creation-Evolution Conflict,* op. cit., pp. 219-220.

28. Ian T. Taylor, *In the Minds of Men*, op. cit., p. 425.

29. Quoted by Henry M. Morris, *The Troubled Waters of Evolution* (San Diego, CA: Creation-Life Publishers, 1974), p. 58. Available from

ICR.

30. Will Durant, "Are We in the Last Stage of a Pagan Period?" (*Chicago Tribune*, April 1980); quoted in Henry M. Morris, *The Long War Against God*, op. cit., p. 149.

31. Henry M. Morris, The Long War Against God (Grand Rapids, MI: Baker Book House, 1989). Ian T. Taylor, In The Minds of Men, 3rd edition (Ontario, Canada: TFE Publishing, 1991).

32. Carl Wieland, "Darwin's Bodysnatchers" (Creation Ex Nihilo, Vol. 14, No. 2, March-May 1992). For further information, contact *Creation Magazine* (P.O. Box 710039, Santee, CA 92072) or Carl Wieland (Director, Creation Science Foundation, Brisbane, Australia). *Creation Magazine* and the Institute for Creation Research should both have Carl Wieland's address.

33. Ibid.

34. Dr. Michael Girouard discusses the relationship between evolution and teenage suicide in the video "Ape Men: Monkey Business Falsely Called Science," which is available through ICR.

35. Kenneth Ham and Gary Parker, Understanding Genesis Study Guide, (El Cajon, CA: Creation Life Publishers, Inc., 1988), p. 4. This book and the video series that it accompanies are available through ICR.

36. Dick Eastman, *University of the World* (Ventura, CA: Regal Books, 1983), pp. 26-27.

PHOTO CREDITS

Dedication Page: Eric Liddell Winning 400-Meter Race (Olympic Games at the Colombes Stadium) on July 19, 1924; © Underwood & Underwood/Corbis; used with permission.

Page 43: Betsie ten Boom; taken from *In My Father's House;* used with permission from The Corrie ten Boom House Foundation, Haarlem, Holland.

Page 49: United States Holocaust Memorial Museum, courtesy of Maria Pfeiffer Virginia Watson Jones (Estate); used with permission.

Page 50: United States Holocaust Memorial Museum United States Holocaust Memorial Museum, courtesy of Richard Freimark William O. McWorkman; used with permission.

Page 54: National Archives and Records Administration, College Park Instytut Pamieci Narodowej Panstwowe Muzeum Auschwitz-Birkenau w Oswiecimiu; public domain.

Page 106: Used with permission from Sinisa Botas at Bigstockphoto.com.

Page 112: From the personal collection of Georgi Vins' daughter, Natasha Velichkin; used with permission (taken from *The Gospel in Bonds* by Georgi Vins, Lighthouse Trails, 2014).

Page 140: ©Eric Liddell Centre; used with permission (www.ericliddell.org).

Page 150: Swedish steamship S/S Vega painted by Jacob Hägg (1839-1931); in the public domain.

Page 154: Used with permission from Michal Bednarek at Bigstockphoto.com.

Page 159: Used with permission from balaikin2009 at Bigstockphoto.com.

Page 160: Used with permission from Michal Bednarek at Bigstockphoto.com.

Page 168: Used with permission from Sinisa Botas at Bigstockphoto.com.

Index

Index

Index

Index

totalitarianism 51
traditional values 28
traumatic experiences 112, 148, 165
tribulations 76, 77, 92
TV 12, 28, 31, 39, 56, 63, 129, 174, 177
Twilight movies 63
tyrannical socialism 57

U

United Nations 12, 55, 56, 58, 129
Universal National Service Act 60
universities 25, 38, 64, 129, 169, 172, 174
University of Delaware 25, 26, 27
University of Minnesota 27
U.S. Justice Department 57
USSR 112
utopian matriarchy 170

V

values clarification 13, 30
video game 31, 32
video games 32, 63
Vins, Pastor Georgi 112, 119
violence 22, 29, 30, 33, 56
Violent video games 32
Virginia Beach 29, 31, 32
Voodoo 44

W

Wagner's operas 170
Wald, George 162, 185
war 18, 28, 40, 43, 57, 108, 140, 145, 171
watered-down Gospel 38
weather 40
Wedgewood Baptist Church 18
Western world 40, 138
Whitcom, John C. 195
white supremacist 25
Wicca 15, 44, 64, 171, 172
Wiccan beliefs 39
Wiccan Goddess 171
Wiccans 169

Other Important Books by Lighthouse Trails

Strength for Tough Times by Maria Kneas
"Another Jesus" Calling by Warren B. Smith
A Time of Departing by Ray Yungen
Faith Undone by Roger Oakland
The Other Side of the River by Kevin Reeves
The Gospel in Bonds by Georgi P. Vins
Trapped in Hitler's Hell by Anita Dittman with Jan Markell
Castles in the Sand and *Dangerous Illusions*
by Carolyn A. Greene and Zach Taylor
Things We Couldn't Say by Diet Eman
In My Father's House by Corrie ten Boom
The Color of Pain by Gregory Reid
Out of India by Caryl Matrisciana
Seducers Among Our Children by Patrick Crough

For a complete listing of Lighthouse Trails books, DVDs, CDs, and more, visit our website at www.lighthousetrails.com. You may also request a catalog by writing to the address on the following page or requesting one at www.lighthousetrails.com/catalog.htm.